Letters on Motherhood

Letters on Motherhood

Giovanna Fletcher

MICHAEL JOSEPH
an imprint of
PENGUIN BOOKS

MICHAEL JOSEPH

UK | USA | Canada | Ireland | Australia
India | New Zealand | South Africa

Michael Joseph is part of the Penguin Random House group of companies
whose addresses can be found at global.penguinrandomhouse.com

First published 2020
001

Copyright © Giovanna Fletcher, 2020

The moral right of the author has been asserted

Set in 14/18.5 pt Garamond MT Std
Typeset by Jouve (UK), Milton Keynes
Printed and bound in Great Britain by Clays Ltd, Elcograf S.p.A.

A CIP catalogue record for this book is available from the British Library

ISBN: 978–0–241–39859–3

www.greenpenguin.co.uk

MIX
Paper from
responsible sources
FSC® C018179

Penguin Random House is committed to a
sustainable future for our business, our readers
and our planet. This book is made from Forest
Stewardship Council® certified paper.

To my three little loves and the men you'll become.
I will forever be yours,

Love, Mumma xxx

CONTENTS

Contents

THE BOOK OF LETTERS . . .

Dear Buzz, Buddy and Max,

When I was pregnant with each of you I used to write you letters. Your dad and I would
take it in turns to
scribble in a book when
we got into bed at night.
The books themselves
weren't anything
special – they'd always be
empty notebooks we
already had in the house –
but we'd write about our
day, what was going on in
our lives and highlight key
moments. Like telling
people about being pregnant

with you, scans, how my body was coping and first kicks. It was a good way for us to document what was happening at that time, and for us to focus on each of you and wonder what life would be like when you arrived.

Those books are yours to keep (you have one each). I'll be honest here: sometimes I was so tired my writing might be illegible, and Max, sadly yours is half the length of Buzz's, but that's being the third child for you. Looking after Buzz and Buddy (and trying to cram in my work) left me so knackered I was too tired to write an entry most nights, but that's no reflection of my unconditional love for you. If we ever go for a fourth child, we'll be asking you three to write the letters instead, because otherwise your sibling will get a blank book!

The first entry in Buzz's book was the start of our path to becoming your parents. I'd already gone through a miscarriage, and a huge part of me was scared I wouldn't get to hold you in my arms either. I always knew I wanted to write letters to you before you were born and beyond but I waited until I was over fourteen weeks pregnant to start, just in case. I had to wait for a time when I felt safe, when I had higher hopes that you'd one day be reading them, even

if you were going to find them highly embarrassing. My heart was already full of love and hope for you, and I was worried that by writing to you I was tempting Fate. I no longer believe in such nonsense. I actually think writing earlier and voicing those thoughts would've helped me process my fears a lot quicker. It would've helped me deal with my anxiety over carrying you. But not to worry, we're all here now.

Writing letters, for me, is a therapeutic way to reflect on the past, be in the present and hope for the future. Motherhood is a massive part of who I am, so I thought I would start writing letters to you and

others in my life who've got me to this point, and who give me the drive to fill our future with happiness.

We don't say how we feel or talk about matters of the heart often enough. We don't unashamedly share our hopes and fears.

Life is so busy – even your young lives are jam-packed with school, nursery, playdates and parties – and sometimes it's just nice to stop and write. There's something so magical about letters and the way they capture a particular moment or thought – even if that thought is a fleeting one, it's bound for ever and shared.

I'm a total sucker for over-sharing: once I start saying how I feel or what I'm doing, I can't stop. At birthdays and Christmas I can't just sign my name in a card and leave it at that. I gush over the recipient – all my thoughts and feelings come tumbling out as I thank them for being who they are and shower them with love.

So, enjoy these letters. These encapsulated thoughts. These ponderings and findings.

Some are for you, and some for others: the other mums who find themselves burying their faces in the kitchen cupboard, feeling overwhelmed, tired and desperate to be enough – unsure whether to laugh or cry, and needing to know they're not on their own. They aren't.

There'll be some sense in there. There'll be some nonsense too. I hope there'll be things in my letters that'll help you understand my past and how I came to be yours.

Love you,
Mumma xxx

LOVE CHANGES

Dear Boys,

You probably don't really think about the love between your dad and me. I imagine it's a bit of a

 weird concept to think of a love being shared that's different from the love we have for you. Seeing as you were born out of that love, I feel I should delve a little deeper into our history, and how things have developed over the last twenty-one years.

On my first day at Sylvia Young Theatre School
I was ushered into a studio of one hundred and fifty
excited children, all giddy at being back at school with
their mates after the summer holidays. I was bang on
time after power-walking from the station, thanks to
a delayed train, and was feeling anxious and nervous
at being the new kid.

My year group, all twenty-two of Year Nine, were
sitting lengthways across the hall in the middle of the
other classes.

Christine, the matron, took my name and led me to
my 'spot', which correlated with the alphabetical place
my name fell in the register. I was placed next to your
dad and his friend Jason Green. There was something
instantly likeable about your dad. Perhaps it was the
way his pink cheeks constantly looked like they were
blushing, the way his silky blond hair fell into perfect
curtains either side of his face, or the fact he was
wearing the cheekiest of grins and his eyes shone as
he spoke to me.

'What's your name?' he asked, Jason smirking
beside him, egging him on.

'Giovanna, but you can call me Gi,' I replied,
already aware that most people couldn't say
'Giovanna' correctly and often forgot it.

'Well, my name's Tom, but you can call me T,' he said, his grin growing wider.

It was cheesy and silly, but at thirteen years old I thought it was super-cute and funny. I giggled in reply, instantly aware that I fancied him. Two minutes into life in a new school and I'd already kick-started a new chapter of teenage drama and love.

Later on that day your dad and a few of the boys in class realized that if they jiggled the letters in my name around you can spell 'vagina'. Embarrassingly I didn't even know how to spell it, and told them they were wrong because there was no *r* in my name – 'virgina' . . . What a tit. Your dad was not deterred, though: we became girlfriend and boyfriend later on that day. According to him I stomped into the courtyard and grabbed him for a kiss in front of everyone, and even stuck my tongue in his mouth, but I don't buy that in the slightest. I was going to say I didn't have much kissing experience back then, but I've suddenly remembered the parties in Year Eight where the goal was to kiss as many guys as possible in that one night (gross) so maybe your dad is right!

Your dad will say he knew instantly in our first conversation that we had a connection and would get married one day. I'm not as adamant as him on that

subject, but there was a definite connection that followed us through the years and kept pulling us back together through the tougher times. From the ages of thirteen to eighteen we were very much an on/off couple, declaring our love for each other, then ballsing it up, causing us to part for some time before we got close again. Not a month went by when we weren't in touch in some way, whether it was by meeting up (it would inevitably end with a kiss), or through texts, calls and emails. Even apart we were still linked.

Fast forward to 2003, the month before I started an

acting degree at Rose Bruford College, and I went to
Namibia for a month to do some charity work with an
orphanage. I had no access to a phone during that
stay. I was cut off from life back home, and I'd
regularly think of your dad. I didn't think too much of
it. I was missing his eighteenth-birthday party, and just
assumed it was my brain's way of processing our
relationship. At that point I'd been with my boyfriend
at the time, a Metropolitan Police officer, for just over
a year. Yet it was your dad who was on my brain.

My boyfriend was pretty uninterested in my life at
drama school, whereas your dad thought it was cool
that I'd moved away from home and was becoming
more independent. For the first five weeks I crashed
on my mate Tom Hopper's sofa in the week and went
home at weekends while I waited for my own
accommodation to be sorted.

It was only when I was driving over to my
boyfriend's house one Friday night, three weeks into
drama school, that I decided I was going to end
things. I hadn't even considered it until that moment,
but it entered my head like some sort of an epiphany
and I felt no doubt or reluctance about doing it. I was
heartbroken knowing that I'd hurt him (I spent the
night cradling his weeping head in my arms) and that

it was likely to be the end of our friendship, but there wasn't a moment of hesitation, which was why I knew it was the right thing to do.

The following weekend your dad asked me to go around to the band house he'd moved into while I was in Namibia. I declined, thinking it was too soon, but agreed to go over the next weekend.

They had a beautiful home in North London, and the boys lived like students with money – eating far too many takeaways, dabbling in weed. They were obsessed with the Xbox. That said, there was an exciting buzz and energy in the place, with musical instruments everywhere and incredible amounts of talent. The times they would just sit there strumming guitars and singing their songs with such emotion and feeling blew me away. The birth of McFly was a magical thing to witness.

On meeting the other boys in the band it was clear they'd been given the lowdown on our history and that your dad was still talking about me. A lot. He and I hung out and caught up. I can remember us driving to Tesco (we were always in Tesco back then) and him buying a bottle of Moët champagne for £20, and having a little chuckle to myself at the ridiculousness of being so grown-up as we drank it with a takeaway

from Pizza Go-go. Time with your dad was effortless and familiar. We just seemed to fit.

A couple of weeks later I moved into my flat in Footscray, near Sidcup. It was small, had damp on the walls, and the couple upstairs constantly had massive rows, but I loved it. The first letter that arrived was from your dad, asking if I'd be his girlfriend again. That was over sixteen years ago.

Two months after we started dating, McFly were featured on a huge Saturday-morning TV show called

CD:UK, and it was instantly obvious that him being a pop star was going to have an impact on our lives. We spent a lot of time apart, living in very different worlds. While your dad was touring the world with his band, I was in drama school pretending to be a penguin.

There have been rocky moments along the way, events that have tested us and shaken us from the ground up – things that are expected when you're growing up alongside one another and learning about the world – but, so far, we've managed to get through it all.

Becoming your parents has deepened the love we have for one another. Of course it's tough. There have been times when we've irritated each other, got snappy or mumbled under our breath as we've walked away. Times when we've been annoyed by the other's ability to block out your calls in the night or protested over needing more sleep when one of you has decided to start your day at five a.m.

But . . .

You boys arriving has shown me a side of your dad I had never seen before. I will not belittle his input into your lives by calling him a 'hands-on dad'. That makes his efforts sound trivial and twee when we're equal and united on all that we give to you. All I will say is the sight of him with you fills me with so much joy and love.

Your dad is my biggest champion and cheerleader, and I respect him more now than ever.

If you grow up and treat your partners with the same love, dedication and compassion that your dad gives me, I'm going to be so very proud.

Love you,
Mumma xx

MY SUNSHINE AND SHOWERS KID

Dear Buddy, or anyone who is fortunate enough to have a child just like you . . .

I've just been following you walking through our hotel in Florida and had a little chuckle to myself in your wake. You had a meltdown on the monorail about not being with me (it was busy so we had to separate for a whole three minutes). Just moments after we were reunited, you went on to have another outburst, this time about not being with your dad. Then a further tantrum erupted when I took you down one level in a lift when you would've preferred to take the stairs.

Reunited with your dad, you were still in meltdown
mode. Some watching you will have been thinking
you were absolutely shattered after a day in the parks,
and I'll admit that probably did contribute to this
particular episode, but let's not pretend it was a one-
off. There was the time I peeled a banana the wrong
way, another when I sliced your toast into cute
triangles when you wanted solid squares, and again
when I refused to let you have ice-cream for
breakfast. And the time you wanted to wear Buzz's
ballet shorts to nursery, your yellow shorts for the
third day in a row, go out with a dozen pairs of pants
on your head, and again when you refused to put on
any clothes at all. Then there was the time I read a
book in the wrong tone of voice, sang too loudly in
the car, danced in the kitchen, and again when I took
a bite out of my crumpet – even though you had your
own on your plate. And the times I lifted you into
your car seat when you wanted to climb up yourself,
when I wouldn't let you drive the car all the way to
Nonno's (or anywhere), and one simply because *I*
picked you up from nursery instead of your dad. And
let's not get started with brushing your teeth, which
seems like the biggest cause of annoyance for you
right now . . .

Yes, you're prone to a little wobble and that outcry in Florida was like any other.

I took a deep breath and walked behind you, following you outside.

I'm not exaggerating when I say that about ten seconds later I watched you in your daddy's arms, dancing and laughing in the rain. You flicked your head back and completely erased the previous ten minutes with your infectious giggle.

You are a complex little soul.

You're emotional in a very different way from Buzz, and your stubbornness has been there from the moment you were born. We always knew what you wanted: even when you couldn't speak you were able to communicate with such focus and determination that we were left in little doubt. Perhaps it's your decisive stubbornness that makes your eruptions seem more explosive than Buzz's ever were, but back then we only had him to focus on. You have a bit more to contend with.

Being a toddler is tough, but these testing flickers of your personality are nothing more than one tiny piece of your puzzle for which there are millions.

So I shall walk behind you (beside you – wherever you blooming want me to), because it's those

complexities that make you so fascinating and
enticing. And above that, you're learning, and in a
world where people don't express themselves enough,
I know it's important for you to work out the feelings
that tamper with your reasonable side.

    This, too, shall pass.

    The good, the bad.

    This, too, shall pass.

    I've learnt to soak up the love when you give it,

drink up the laughs when you spill them and marvel at the warmth of your hand when you place it in mine.

You are totally unpredictable. I love you and your craziness, my sunshine and showers boy.

Love,

your Mumma xxx

THREE LITTLE WORDS,
ONE BROKEN HEART

Dear Buzz,

You were barely a year old when you first told me you loved me. You were learning to talk and I was telling you I loved you all the time, something I still say repeatedly to you and your brothers, so it's hardly surprising that you pieced together something that sounded remotely like 'I love you'. To anyone else I'm sure it would've been standard gobbledegook, nothing to report, but I was thrilled and jumped on the moment. I was literally on cloud nine. You were saying the 'words' I longed to hear. I'm not entirely sure you knew the power of those little words but hearing you say them filled me with the greatest joy.

This morning, though, you said the words I always feared you'd say. And I deserved it. It was 5.15 a.m. when you and your brother came wandering into our room. You haven't quite mastered volume control yet and you've never been fans of a lie-in (Oh, how I miss still being in bed until 8 a.m.). Max was asleep and your dad had been poorly. You wanted to tell me that you'd just managed to read the start of one of your night-time books all by yourself. I didn't listen to you and took you both back to your room while trying to explain you had to be quiet. People were sleeping. You ignored me and bounced around in your usual energetic way. I asked you to calm down and go back to sleep.

You wanted to carry on reading. I wanted you to lie down and shut your eyes. It was 5.17 a.m. I'd already been up to feed Max in the night. It was your third morning of waking up at this time and you get so emotional when you've not slept well. There's always a knock-on effect to these early starts. I wish you could see that.

Neither of us was willing to compromise so we fell out. I took the book, snatching it, and threw it across the room. My sudden movement scared you and, in response, you shouted at me with such anger, a scratching in your throat as the words made their way out of your mouth.

'I hate you.'

Ouch.

I cried when you left the room (your dad came to get you after overhearing us) and I felt like a failure. I should've been calmer. I should've listened to you and praised you for the achievement you were so proud of.

I felt so ashamed. I've been mulling over those feelings today. I hate getting angry because it reminds me of parts of my childhood where I would've been aggravated and unsure how to communicate those feelings. I used to have so much anger inside me as a kid and in my teens. I have to link it to my hearing difficulties during the first couple of years, as well as being part of an Italian/Essex family, which meant we were also quite explosive at times. I shrugged that off at drama school as I became more aware of my emotions, triggers, and how my actions affected others. On the whole I'm far more laidback now and my feathers aren't ruffled easily, but frustration and tiredness got the better of me this morning and really shouldn't have done. No matter how depleted I feel, I never want to make you scared or angry. It breaks my heart thinking of it like that. You're the sweetest, bubbliest little boy. I'm your mother and am here to give you love, support and comfort.

The sad thing is I know you're not always going to like me. As a family there will be times when boundaries are put in place that you disagree with, or when we clash over things, but I hope we find a way to use our words, understand and listen.

I don't want to be the one spoiling your fun. I don't want to be the one nagging you about doing homework or getting your shoes and socks on so we can leave the house. I don't want to be the one telling you not to do the things you desperately want to do. But I am and I will be, because I'm your mother. I will continue to do all of those things that make you huff and moan at me. I'll carry on because it is my job to love you and care for you, and to worry constantly about your safety, your heart and your future.

So, yes, sometimes I get angry at the silliest of things, but I think it's because the silliest of things set you off, which causes me to wobble. Part of me is already panicking about what lies ahead and how we'll manage if you won't listen to me even in insignificant situations. I feel lost, overwhelmed and panicked. I have to remind myself that what's unimportant to me might mean the world to you, and even if it doesn't, even if you've just become fixated on something because you're tired or upset, that's OK. Because you are learning, and it's my job to give you reassurance and guidance as you do so.

But also . . . Sometimes, I'm just knackered and I break. I snap. I fracture. I shatter. I'm so weighed down by the mothering load, the external pressures and having to stay on top of it all that I burst. I combust, and the fallout of that explosion crushes me, because you are my all.

I'm so sorry.

There has been a heaviness in my chest today, and tonight I'm going to bed telling myself I must do better. I want you to know that I'm trying my best, even if sometimes I make mistakes and do the wrong thing. I'm learning. I want to be the best mum I can be. You deserve that.

Love you always – and I'm so very proud of your reading!
Mumma xxx

YOUR HANDS

For Buddy,

I'm not sure what it is about your hands,
But I've always loved them,
Also been so glad
When you've slipped them into mine,
Your pads sitting so warmly,
So sturdy.
Little *doing* hands,
Hands ready for adventure,
Ready to seize the day
And find their way.

The way a palm can cup your little chin,
Your head cocked to the left,
Your ears listening.
Your eyes doeful,

Letters on Motherhood

Full of expression,
As you take in a story with wonder and awe.
All the meltdowns from the day
I'm ready to ignore.

Your little hands,
Whether gesturing or relaxing,
They capture my attention,
Pausing my worries.
See, right now your brain is muddled,
Thinks it needs to argue.
It makes you headstrong,
Stubborn and fiery.

But,
Your hands,
They show me who you really are,
How much you have to offer
And that you will go far.
You'll cherish this world,
Nurture those who need it.
Yes, you'll fight when it's needed,
But give mostly love.
Yes, I believe it.

Dear Buzz, Buddy and Max,

When I was at primary school and I was just seven years old, I was badly bullied by two girls in my year. It started with name-calling – I would be told that I was fat or that I smelt. It escalated until I was being tripped up or pushed – I remember three occasions when I was shoved backwards into rose bushes, which resulted in the school nurse having to pull thorns out of my bum cheeks. It's something I'll

29

never forget. Even now the sight of rose bushes is enough to make me shudder.

I'd known the girls involved for a few years before the trouble started. They were constantly over at each other's houses and their mums were very close. I desperately wanted to be part of their team. I wanted in on their fun. They were a duo, though, and I was most certainly the third wheel – like an eager puppy looking for love and validation. When they argued, one of them would fuss over me to make the other jealous, and I was quickly dropped when they reconciled. When I tried to make other friends, they'd be warned away. There was a hierarchy and these girls had all the power over me and my peers.

I felt so alone. I started playing ball games with the boys because things seemed so much simpler with them. Everyone was allowed. It was nicer to play with a ball than have someone playing with me. Of course, you know I'm not the best at catching or throwing, so the other thing I did when I found myself playing on my own was walk around the field singing to myself and acting out little scenes. My imagination took me away from what was happening with others and led me elsewhere. Little did anyone know I was exercising the muscles I would go on to use in my writing. It's nice to think that I'm now living the silver lining to what was a very tough time.

The bullying didn't stop. Things didn't blow over. My mum found out and marched me up to the school on several occasions, demanding to know what they were going to do about it. Schools didn't have anti-bullying policies back then, and there was little in place to stop children feeling isolated or excluded. My teacher, who I remember being a very sweet and gentle woman, was powerless to help.

I don't blame Mum for getting involved, and I don't think I was ever embarrassed by her. I just wanted it all to stop and the girls to like me. I can only imagine how heartbreaking it must've been for Mum. It was her job to protect me from harm and keep me happy – yet the behaviour of those girls was out of her control. After two years we needed a break, so we moved to a lovely village in Essex called Ingatestone. I'm not sure whether that move would always have happened, but I did feel a big part of the decision to up sticks was down to me and those girls, and the horrible drama that surrounded it.

Mum and Dad moved us to somewhere more rural, and I'm thrilled they did. My new school was tiny in comparison to the one before, and my love

of music led to me flourishing through song. I
felt free.

I'd like to say that what I experienced as a seven-
year-old was my only run-in with bullying, but that's
not the case. When I was twelve or thirteen some
'friends' would do this strange thing where they'd eat
chocolate (a Penguin bar, to be precise), then put
water in their mouths and spit at me. My yellow
blouse would be brown and mucky. I'm sure they
would've said it was just a laugh, but it didn't feel
very funny to be on the receiving end of it. It was
just one of the many games they would play at
my expense.

Fortunately I wasn't going to be sticking around in
that school for much longer as I was heading to Sylvia
Young Theatre School, where I would meet your dad.
There would still be drama (mostly with your dad),
but I found a group of people who were focused on
our combined joy – performing. Days spent there
were happy, and I would practically jump out of bed in
the mornings eager to start doing something I loved.
I felt incredibly grown-up and independent when I
was travelling alone into London on the train and
tube – which must've been tough for my parents to
allow. They knew it was something I wanted to do,

though. After all, it was me who'd seen Sylvia Young
on *Live and Kicking* and decided to phone up her school
for a prospectus. It was me who decided to apply for a
scholarship and only tell my parents what I'd done
when a date came through to audition. My mum and
dad knew nothing about the world I was venturing
into, but they let me find out where applying would
take me. I think we were all a little shell-shocked
when I was actually offered a place.

I'm glad they let me go.

I'd like to think that, as you grow and start chasing

your own dreams, we'll be able to support you in the same way my parents did me.

Your school years are so important, and as you boys go off through those gates, make friends and gain your own independence, I'll be thinking of seven-year-old me and all she went through. I'll wonder if you're happy, if people are being good to you, if we've made the right decisions for you, and whether any moments will shape who you later become. I'll fight with myself over asking you too many questions about your day and who you were with, tell myself it's OK if you play by yourself occasionally, remind myself that it's good you're not seeking approval from others in the way I once did – but also that it's natural to want to be part of a collective, to be liked.

You will find your way.

Perhaps more than my worries over how others might treat you (I know it's out of my control: all I can do is give you the tools and support you need to deal with it), I have found myself wondering how you might treat others. Will you be inclusive? Will you go to the kid sitting on their own and include them in a game? Will you stand up for someone being mistreated? Will you actively seek to make someone's day a little brighter? Or will you go blindly through life as though you're the most important one, disregarding the feelings of others? Will you ever treat others in the way I was once treated?

I hope not.

Words are powerful.

Please use yours to encourage, support and empower those who deserve it. If in doubt, take a step back in the hope of seeing things a little more clearly.

Love you,
Mumma xxx

HEARD FROM THE FRONT SEAT — ON MY OWN

You're squabbling over your Marvel figures. Captain America has been dropped on the floor and is now out of reach. You're fighting over the remaining Ant-Man and Hulk, while Max is busy gurgling with Spider-Man. Instead of stepping in for the hundredth time, I've decided to see how you tackle the situation.

Buddy: I'm going on my own. I'm going to get a car and drive it myself. I'm going to the shop and I'm going to get crisps and then I'm going to the sweetie shop and I'm going to buy chocolate.

Buzz: Well, then, I'll have all your toys.

Buddy: I'm not going to get toys, Buzz. I'm going to eat everything . . . (*Pause while he processes the argument.*) You're a booboobuttfoot.
You both descend into cackling laughter.
Crisis averted.

Dearest Buzz and Buddy,

I'm currently lying in bed with you, Buddy. The red,
blue and green stars from your light are twirling
above us and, if I'm honest, they're a bit too fast for
my liking. I wonder if they're set at that speed to
prompt dizziness, forcing you to close your eyes
and get to sleep.

Buzz, you're fast asleep – which I find surprising
as I had to tell you off only a few minutes ago for
jumping on your bed. It amazes me how you and
your brothers have the ability to flit between emotions
and states of being so quickly. From high energy to
snoozing in seconds. You're a wonder.

Buddy, you're being adorable and hugging my arm.
This is very new for you as you've never been one for
snuggles. On the very rare occasions that you've

crawled into our bed, you've let us know that you're there to sleep, not to be touched or fussed over. We know to leave you be: even when you've fallen over and hurt yourself, it's very rare for you to seek comfort from us. But that's you. You pick yourself up and get on with life – too busy exploring to worry over a graze or bump.

Something has definitely kicked in with you lately, though, as you've started to give the sweetest kisses and really hold us tightly in cuddles – not in the dominant headlock type of way that I'd expect from you, but a really loving embrace that melts my heart.

For the last few evenings you've looked up at me as I've been tucking you in and asked me to get into your bed. I know, warning bells should've sounded. They did. 'It's a rod, a rod for your back. Don't do it. Do not get into that bed. You'll be paying for that bit of affection for months.' I paused before responding, swimming in your big brown eyes as they implored me to stay. There was no way I was leaving and so I enjoyed the warmth of your arms as I slid in next to you.

You're currently trying to get yourself off to sleep but you had a danger nap earlier. You fell asleep while hugging me (again! Another hug!) on the sofa at

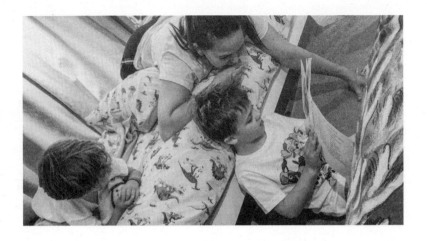

3.30 p.m. after an active morning. Warning bells
sounded then, too, and I knew there'd be
consequences tonight, but I was enjoying the peace
that came with it a little too much. With Buzz resting
on my other arm, even I closed my eyes and relaxed
into a cheeky snooze. Bliss. Moments like that are
what I thought motherhood would be like. Calm,
loving, and heartwarming – if it weren't for all of our
clothes being covered with snot, crumbs and mud,
and my make-up-less face being framed by my halo of
postpartum hair, we'd be fit enough for a picture-
perfect shot of parenthood expectations. I never
realized that moment felt so good because it came
after chaos, shouting and frantic playing.

As predicted, I'm paying for that glorious nap now. I wanted to go for a run tonight . . . It's already 8.45 p.m. Maybe I should dig out a headtorch . . . You'll fall asleep soon enough. I'll just wait. No sense in getting annoyed. I accepted the love in a hug, and now I'm here to stay.

As a parent I find myself torn between 'doing what's best' for you, in terms of what the experts say is good for you and your development, and just enjoying the moment. From the moment I became a mum it seemed everyone had an opinion on what I should be doing in every area of motherhood – from breastfeeding to sleeping, to the use of a pacifier and even where I put you to nap. Everyone had some nugget of advice to give. At first I tried to take it all on board, remembering what the books had said while listening to family and friends, or even strangers who'd accosted me on the street. It was all conflicting and confusing. I had to banish the lot from my brain and slowly tune in to my own maternal instincts, which I hadn't been able to hear over their advice.

I always say to expectant mums to listen to all the advice being thrown at them and then forget it. It's the only way of finding what works for them and their families without endlessly looking over their shoulders for approval. That's definitely what I've found with you guys. We've found a way that's not right and not wrong: it just works for us.

I'm so glad I enjoyed the moment this afternoon (who knows when you'll both use me as a pillow again?), and I'm smitten over the moment we're sharing right now . . . even if I am making notes into my phone to ensure I never forget it.

Love you,
Your Mumma — the woman who will always be waiting with open arms for that hug

REDUCED TO TEARS BY
A STRANGER

To the Swimming Interrupter,

Because he'd been listening, helpful around the house,
and staying in bed until his Groclock said it was time
to wake up, Buddy's reward jar was full to the brim
with multi-coloured stars. As a treat I decided to take
him for a swim after dropping Buzz off at school.
Max was at home with Tom so it was
just me and Buddy, my
three-year-old, who
rarely gets me all to
himself, just like I never
get him all to myself. Tom
had taken him swimming
a few times since I'd had
Max, and I knew he loved
doing that because he loves

the pool on holidays and was getting very confident in the water.

Buddy was a little grouchy when he woke up that morning but, then, we all have days when we feel groggy first thing. He was super-happy at the drop-off and telling everyone we were going swimming. He listened to me when we were crossing the gym car park, held my hand and stayed by my side as we paid to go in. He was excited as we got changed into our costumes. He laughed at how his Hulk swimsuit meant he was wearing purple shorts, even though it was just a print on the all-in-one Lycra suit. He popped the 50p into the locker, helped me with the towels and practically skipped to the side of the pool.

This was where the switch was flicked.

The kids' pool – a pool he never usually went into – was closed for private lessons, meaning we'd have to go in the bigger pool. This displeased Buddy, who was adamant on going into the kids' one. He sat on the side of the pool, legs dangling into the water, and cried big fat tears.

I tried reasoning with him, explaining that it was closed for the bigger children and their teachers. I used the lifeguard as some sort of security figure perching up high on his chair who wouldn't let us

in – when in truth he was giving us a bit of judgemental side eye. I tried laughing and showing him how much fun the water was, trying to create a game for him to enjoy. It was all useless as he couldn't hear me over his continual wailing loop of 'I want to go in da ovvur poool' as his little hand reached out to his dream destination.

I was trying.

Then you appeared.

'Do you mind if I say something?' you asked, your voice clipped.

You'd been swimming – the calm experience probably ruined by our arrival.

I just stared at you, my mind not quick to shift from the exchange with my son. It's not often people interrupt in situations like this – or maybe they don't usually ask first. I'm used to a 'We've all been there' interaction, but your focus was on Buddy, not me.

'You know, it's the same water as in here. It's the same,' you told him, splashing the water with your cupped hand.

A new voice. We all know that's what it takes sometimes. Someone other than their parent telling them the exact same thing – giving it some validation. A little distraction to pull them back into the now and away from the focus of your threenager's determined mind. Usually I 'find' a fox or horse in the garden to get excited about, which conveniently runs off when he's turned to look, and then we try to find it together, completely forgetting about the desire or need that's been left behind – no longer important.

I'd had no such luck with my distraction techniques,

but you seemed to have an effect. Buddy stopped moaning and shied away, curling into himself – which I knew meant he still wasn't happy but you had at least broken the spell.

To be honest, I was glad of the peace, as I'm sure others were too.

You then turned to me. 'You see, sometimes they just need a new voice. To explain things in a different way.'

Yup.

'He's very intelligent. You just need to try different ways so that he can grasp what you're saying.'

Yup.

That's what I was doing.

'I've got four boys. All grown-up now. My eldest is twenty,' you continued.

I didn't think to tell you that I had two other boys at home, as I started to get the impression you didn't think much of my mothering skills – the brief glimpses of which you'd caught as you were swimming past.

You then turned your attention back to Buddy – I'd managed to get him into the pool because he was cold. He clung to my side. You heard him mumble that he still wanted to go into the other pool. Part of me was a little happy that your pep talk had failed, that

you could see what I was working with – a child who knows his own mind and is super-stubborn to boot.

'Oh,' you said, as though realizing something you'd previously omitted. 'Is he tired?' The simple sentence was loaded with judgement, as though I was failing him at bedtime too.

In that moment my patience with you waned, even though I knew you were only trying to be helpful.

'He's three,' was my matter-of-fact reply. 'He's being a three-year-old.'

'Hmm . . .'

'I want to go in da ovvur pooool,' Buddy said again, albeit at a lower volume, as he fiddled with my costume.

You then came up with an elaborate plan for me to go into the other pool and have him ask the children their ages, stating that if they were older than him (they were school age), he couldn't possibly go in there because he was too small.

You looked up at me and said, 'Is that too much work, Mummy?' As though I was being lazy in my approach.

I smiled in reply.

I'll be honest, there was no way I was going to interrupt a private class of children and start asking them questions. I was humiliated enough and am pretty sure strangers talking to children when they're half naked is frowned upon. Regardless, I asked Buddy if he wanted to go and see what the other children were doing – another tactic with him, and I also wanted to run away from you. I thanked you, we got out, and you carried on swimming.

After a few seconds of standing and watching as their teacher shouted at them, Buddy declared he needed a wee. Of course he did, because he'd refused to go before we got into the pool, like I'd suggested.

So, dripping wet, we went to the only available loo – a changing-room combo of a cubicle, which was currently occupied. We could hear someone showering inside so they weren't coming out any time soon.

You appeared again.

'Oh, are you giving up?'

'He just needs a wee.'

You nodded. 'It's so important to explain to them in a way they understand. He's very intelligent,' you reiterated, repeating your earlier comment as you got your bag from your locker. 'I have four boys. I am a more experienced mother. There's no point repeating the same thing over and over. You need to find other ways that they'll understand.'

You wouldn't have noticed my eyes sting at that point as I nodded in reply at you pulling rank. More children, more hours put in – a better mum. No excuses from me, or corrections over my 'methods', just a pathetic nod.

Do you realize that you made me feel like a shit

mum? I already felt it, obviously, but your comment about being more experienced, the way you told me what I should be doing with my child and where I was going wrong – I instantly felt stupid, inept and vulnerable.

The person wasn't coming out of the cubicle yet as the shower was still running, but I politely said goodbye (I didn't want you to think I wasn't exercising good manners with my kids) and took Buddy to the baby changing room instead. There was a sink. He peed in that. I know, I'm disgusted too, but he has an excellent aim and I promise I did a thorough clean-up job afterwards.

Buddy, now calm but quite reserved with his blotchy red face, asked to go back by the pool – he'd spotted another little boy of his age going in with his mummy. Did he want to go in and have fun like the happy little boy? Of course not. Instead I sat on a chair at the side of the pool, both of us wrapped in towels, Buddy on my lap, and watched this little boy and his mummy laughing and giggling.

That was the morning I wanted with my little boy.

I cried into Buddy's hair.

I had failed.

I would've come to that conclusion without your

interruption, but you made me realize that not only did I know I'd failed but others did too. I felt you were voicing the opinions of those who dared not interrupt.

We sat there for five minutes before Buddy decided he wanted to go. He was so cute and chatty while we got dressed and made our way to the car.

I thought of you as we carried on with our tasks, and on the drive home, when I looked in my rear-view mirror to see Buddy sleeping, I cried again.

On the whole I'm sure you meant well. You were only trying to defuse the situation and get him into the pool. That said, you didn't truly take into consideration my feelings as his mother. I know I was internally frustrated at the situation and that could possibly have skewed how I see our exchange. However, part of me is irked that you got my son to calm down (even if you didn't get him into the pool properly) because you, whether knowingly or not, used that as a tool to highlight my incompetence for the rest of our exchange.

I occasionally look at other people with my children and marvel at how wonderful they are at being with them – how brilliantly my children respond to their direction and guidance. That can (just every now and then) leave me feeling inadequate – and I'm their

mum. The truth of the matter is that most children enjoy interactions with adults other than their parents and hang on their every word. It's happened to me with other people's kids before I became a mum, and I know it's made me feel like I was the Pied flipping Piper. But it's a novelty, someone new to look at. Someone who's not going to make you brush your teeth twice a day, put your shoes and socks on even though you want to be barefooted and also tell you it's bedtime when all you really want to do is stay up and play.

It's hardly surprising that I felt truly crap at the end of the day. It was an epic fail of all proportions. Yet, on reflection, maybe there are some positives to be taken from it. I'm happy that I stayed calm and patient with Buddy. That I showed him nothing but love and sympathy. That I didn't snap at him for the day not going as I'd hoped it would (I was a little short with Tom later on, though – I know, totally irrational and unfounded). I'm glad I managed to keep moving forwards.

As the experienced mother you are, you must recognize there are some days where we feel like we've failed, where our parenting toolkit can provide us with nothing of use, where our hearts feel crushed and defeated – where we feel nothing but judgement, shame and guilt even though all we've acted with is love.

With your experience as a mother, you must recognize the importance of language, and how comforting it is to be offered reassurance by other mothers – especially in the middle of a situation with a determined three-year-old.

Experience.

Thank you for our encounter. You've now given me the knowledge, understanding and compassion to ensure I never make another parent feel how I did after you spoke to me.

Your experience as a mother has made such an impact on my own. When I see another parent in a difficult situation, be it a meltdown at the pool or a full-blown tantrum in a supermarket, I will be there to make eye contact, offer words of encouragement, and to reassure them they're doing a good job.

Yes, I'll let them know that I also have kids and experience as a mother, but not in a manner that states authority or judgement.

Instead I'll offer them the empathy, grace and kindness that I could've done with today, letting them know I've been there too. I'll let them know that the outburst I'm seeing has not made me question their mothering skills and that I haven't made snap assumptions. Instead, whatever passes between us, be it a look or a simple 'I've been there', will bolster them through the moment with a bit more ease.

Thanks for giving me such clarity.

Much love,
Giovanna

MY GREATEST SURPRISE

Dearest Max,

I have no shame in saying that I was surprised when I found out I was pregnant with you: 2017 had been an unbelievably busy year, and 2018 was set to be even more intense. My career was really picking up speed. The first series of the *Happy Mum, Happy Baby* podcast, which I had created, had repeatedly hit the top spot in the charts each week, I'd just got back from a charity trek in Oman for CoppaFeel! (and was set to make them

an annual challenge), had achieved fantastic sales for
the publication of my novel *Some Kind of Wonderful*, and
had just finished performing at the Hammersmith
Apollo in a stage production of *The Christmasaurus*
with your dad, Aunty Carrie, Matt Willis and Harry
Judd. (It had felt fantastic to be back on stage.)

Looking back, I can see that I was starting to feel
like 'me' again after losing myself a bit in motherhood.
Buzz and Buddy were my everything – that should go
without saying – but by that point I was able to leave
them with your nana when I needed to so that I could
focus on creating work and engaging in conversations
with adults. I was coming out of the fog.

Life was good. The juggle, although never truly
balanced, seemed to be tentatively working. Yes, I'd
have moments when I felt enormous guilt and worried
whether I was ever being the best mum, wife, friend
I could be – but I was muddling through. I was
getting it done. We were happy. Most of the time.

When we'd finished in *The Christmasaurus* I was
shattered, but also still on a high from the previous
year, and all that was planned for the one ahead.
I remember so clearly that on 3 January I was sitting
on the sofa in the afternoon and suddenly felt very
cold. I was wrapped up in layers under a fluffy blanket,

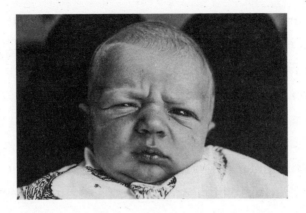

but I was still freezing. The last time I could remember being chilled in that way was when I was pregnant with Buddy. The thought slowly trickled in. Could I be? Surely not . . . Maybe.

I had a pregnancy test in the bathroom (I had bulk-bought them when trying for Buddy, I think) and went off to pee on it to avoid all doubt.

'PREGNANT' appeared on the screen pretty swiftly. I felt sick. I would've told your dad in a fun way (like getting one of your brothers to just wander in to him with the test), but I needed him to know instantly.

We knew we were going to have a third child (or, at least, I definitely did), but your dad had always pulled a funny face about it happening anytime soon, seeing as life was already chaotic. I was never sure whether it was something he did for comic effect when we were with our mates or how he truly felt. He had been reluctant but said he was open to the idea once some time had passed and we were managing to get some sleep.

We'd said we'd wait a couple more years . . .

You had other plans.

My heart was in my mouth as I ran down the stairs to find him. He was in his office with your brother Buzz – they were building Lego and watching *Star Wars*. I felt sick as I ushered your dad out of the room and thrust the test into his hand.

He laughed – a happy, joyous laugh that told me he was thrilled.

I cried.

I was just so flipping knackered.

I had wanted to wait so that I could take time off whenever my third baby arrived. I was actively putting my all into everything so I could get to a point in my career that would allow me to disappear and fully immerse myself in family life without the guilt of work looming overhead.

I was not at that point. I would have to juggle both.

I was already pushed to my mental capacity.

How was I going to get everything done *and* have a baby?

I wasn't crying because I didn't want you. It was the

shock. The sudden halt of plans, and the knowing that my body would be taken over once again, even though I'd just pushed myself into a healthy state of fitness through my training for Oman.

It all sounds so selfish, and it was.

I was in a bit of a daze for the rest of the day.

That night I went onto Instagram and read a post from a lady called Louise, who had given birth to her sleeping baby Gabriel a few weeks earlier. She appeared in my 'recommended feed' and I found myself transfixed by her page as I read about her son and how she had cared for him before taking a strand of his hair to keep in a locket so that he'd always be with her.

That was the reality check I needed.

I wept again. For Louise, for Gabriel, and then for us.

I realized how incredibly lucky I was to have you with me, even in those early stages, when so many women long for the babies they'll never see grow up, or the babies they desperately want but can't have.

Like a bolt of armour being pinged across my body, in an instant the feeling of protection kicked in. My plans might've shifted, but I knew life would go on.

I was being given one more heart to give thanks and love for. What a little miracle.

One thing I didn't factor in was how it would feel

to have another little human loving me back. Max, your love is all-encompassing. You radiate joy. In the morning when you wake up you simply lie there and take in the space around you. When I walk in, your face lights up. When I pick you up, your little arms cling around my neck, giving me the tightest of hugs. And it is a real hug. A happy desire to be close to me, to show me love and affection.

The way you look at your brothers, even when they're being too heavy-handed, loud, or pushing their faces into yours as they make ridiculous noises, is so adoring. You're soaking them up. Lapping up life. You're so happy to be alive.

They say that we adults should try seeing the world through the eyes of a child, and I really wish I could see it through yours.

Max, my happy surprise, you have forced me to slow down, made me question my workload, calmed me, helped me to say no to things that will push me beyond my limits. You've given me back some of my life, simply by being in it. You have completed this family by pulling us closer together than ever before.

Love you,
Mumma xxx

To the lady on the train with the screaming baby,

Please do not apologize that your tiny newborn daughter is crying. Do not try to justify why she's on the train, or make excuses for her tears. Do not talk about how everyone on the tube must hate you for the noise – your forced laughter doesn't hide the wobble in your voice as you avoid eye contact with other passengers and fiddle with the pram. Through the words you say to your daughter,

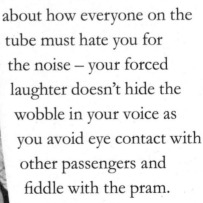

I've learnt you have taken her out of the house and been on an adventure into London. You've been back to your place of work and given her a grand tour of your office space – a meeting of your old world and your new. A day where you realized just how much your life has moved on, just how much your world has changed, yet just how much your old life has remained still and unwavering. It's a collision of two universes that are millions of light years away from one another.

I've been there.

After having my third son, Max, I went to see my management six weeks after he was born. I was in town for my check-ups and their office was on the same road so it made sense to pop in. Tom and Buddy were with us too, so there was lots to juggle, but I thought I was just taking him in to meet everyone so that they could all coo over him and tell me how gorgeous he was – that's it. Don't get me wrong, that was how most of my time there was spent, but there were work things that needed to be discussed too. I might've been on 'maternity leave' but, as I'd arranged, plans were still moving forward for future projects and I had to be across them. And so I listened, nodded, and tried to engage my brain as I bounced a grumpy Max on my knee, while Tom walked an excited Buddy up and down the aisle of the office and tried to avoid a meltdown.

Being with my children in a space that was usually reserved for important business meetings felt so alien. I couldn't focus, couldn't concentrate, and therefore got drenched in mum sweat – it was dripping down my spine as my cheeks flushed. The familiar dirty and hot feeling floored me even though I'd managed to shower and had made an effort that morning with my clothes, had actually washed my hair and added a touch of mascara to my lashes.

Max needed feeding. I'm an old hand at that activity, but suddenly getting my boobs out in an office, in a work space where everyone was getting on with their jobs, felt weird. It made me uneasy.

The two worlds jarred against each other and I felt really uncomfortable around a group of people I love dearly – who would've been mortified if they'd known how I was feeling. You see, it wasn't them really: it was the realization that life was continuing, that at some point I'd need to return to work, and that the juggle of work and motherhood would continue, with one added member to factor into the equation. It was suddenly as though Max was being taken away, and that our time together was being robbed from me.

My brain was screaming at me to get out while my body started to feel as though millions of ants were crawling under my skin, itching to escape.

It was too much too soon.

I left the office feeling crushed and dazed.

I felt 'something other'.

That was the start of me finding myself in a dark place. I was overwhelmed by the demands of the two worlds. And it was only seeing the two of them side by side that I truly understood how much of me they both required, and how big the juggling act was.

I felt out of sorts and I stewed on those feelings,

wondering if I'd ever be comfortable in my old world again, or if the pressure was just too much.

A few weeks later, in maternal mental health week, I scrolled through my feed and saw post after post from women opening up about their experiences of being on the wobble. I felt relieved. I felt empowered. I didn't feel quite so alone, and that made me weep as I sat and wrote my own post to add to the many. Sifting through my thoughts and getting them down on the page was the kindest thing I could've done for myself in that moment. After weeks of saying I was fine, I was able to lift the veil and acknowledge the fuzz in my head:

> *I've not been feeling myself the last couple of weeks, which is pretty tough to admit. I've tried to say it out loud a few times and then totally dismissed it and brushed it under the carpet. I have found myself saying, 'I'm not feeling myself, but it's fine. I'm fine.'*
>
> *Hmm . . .*
>
> *I'm fine but sometimes I don't want to get out of bed in the morning. I don't want to get dressed. I don't want to see people. I don't want to do anything.*
>
> *I'm fine but I've been crying for no reason and occasionally can't seem to stop.*

I'm not feeling myself right now but I've just had a baby and my hormones are all over the shop, playing havoc with my emotions.

I'm not feeling myself right now but I've just welcomed my third baby into the world and am so incredibly lucky.

I'm not feeling myself right now but people are asking things of me and I don't want to let them down. I want to deliver and be the productive, proactive and positive person I usually am.

I'm not feeling myself right now BUT thankfully I have a great bunch of people around me who are giving me lots of support and making sure I'm kinder to myself.

We must be kinder to ourselves! And we must talk.

I wasn't going to add to the amazing conversations happening around mental health today, but seeing as they've all helped me, I thought adding to it might just help some others. Be kinder and talk.

And that's my point. Days of awareness are so important, because they mean someone like me might see honest, heartfelt posts and feel encouraged when it comes to their own situation. They might discover they're not alone in their feelings. They might decide to seek help.

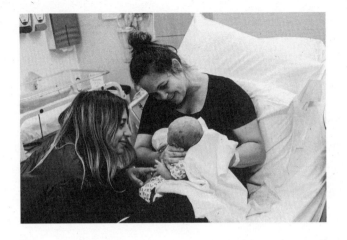

Did you know the leading cause of death in new mums is suicide? I know. It's a heartbreaking fact. It goes to show how important it is to talk freely without sugar-coating everything, how we shouldn't dismiss a mother's feelings as 'baby blues' or be ashamed of the thoughts in our heads or think we need to appear to have everything under control when we don't. Babies (and children) are unpredictable and *that* is fine.

I've always said honesty is the best thing you can give to a new mum, and now I believe that more than ever. Motherhood is hard. When you go back into your place of work and see people milling around desks, holding hot drinks, wondering what they're going to have for lunch at the pub, peeing in peace, wearing clothes that don't have to offer easy boob access, looking like they've not just put them on as an afterthought that morning but actually taken time over and pride in their appearance – doing things that aren't linked to projectile poos or tackling the ever-growing piles of washing – it's like an alien world.

And that is OK.

Life has changed and it's OK to feel confuddled and conflicted as your priorities pivot on a new axis.

It's OK to be drawn towards your old life and feel conflicted by what you find.

Sometimes it's OK not to be OK.

Of course, there is a chance that beyond the moment on the train, you and your daughter had had the most wonderful day. But it reminded me of the first collision of my worlds. So just in case that makes you head home with a depleted heart that feels crushed and lonely – I just wanted you to know it's fine to feel the way you are and I wanted to tell you you're doing a wonderful job.

You really are.

Big love,
Gi xx

To my long-suffering body, the one that gets me through life and has enabled me to become a mother,

Max was only weeks old. I was having a snuggle with Buzz on the sofa (my eldest child was your first amazing gift to me). While I was pregnant, he had marvelled over my growing bump for months, sitting with his hands splayed across the stretched skin, patiently waiting for Max to

move or kick while singing songs to him and whispering words of love.

Now doughy skin lay in the place Max once inhabited. Buzz rested his hands on it, obviously taken aback by the waterbed quality it had acquired since his smallest brother had arrived. 'I love your squidgy tummy,' he said, smiling at it, his eyes full of wonder, as though marvelling at the miracle of life.

Children see things, and then they comment, their words unfiltered. It's kind of like *Catchphrase* but in real life – they have Roy Walker or Steven Mulhern perched on their shoulders egging them on: 'Say what you see, kid. Say what you see.'

When my children look at you they do not see your lumps and bumps, the dimpling of flesh, or the silvery indented lines that look like a snail has slithered all over you. Neither do they think you should be bigger or smaller. When they see you, they see me. We are one.

Their love for me is completely entwined with their love for you. In a crowded space, as their eyes catch sight of me, they feel only happiness, happiness that I am there. That's something to remember next time I'm standing in front of a mirror scrutinizing your appearance.

Through them I am learning to love you, to take care of you and to stop treating you like something I loathe. It's given me time to stop and reassess our relationship, and realize that I've been terrible to you.

I'm sorry.

I'm sorry that when I was twelve I used to share an orange and small bowl of fries with my friend Madz to make you smaller. I'm sorry I used to punch you and to blame you for things outside your control. I'm sorry that I've spent so much of my time disliking you. I failed to see that you were damaged, hurt, and

in need of my love. I never realized your strength. I'm sorry I thought you were only worth loving if you looked different, and that I didn't accept you for so long and take joy in the fact you were mine.

It's funny, I thought I'd hate you more than ever now. Bigger, more stretched, droopier, saggier, more worn, achy and wobbly. I don't. I value you now and only wish I had done so sooner. I know you'll continue to change but I'll do my best to embrace that. There will be days when my mind wobbles and compares you to others but I have finally accepted you and I understand just how special you are.

Big love,
Your mind xx

YOUR HEART

For Buzz.

Do you remember when you were younger?
The way I used to join you
Sitting

     on

          the

               bottom

                    step

Sent there for cheeky behaviour?
Although for what I can't remember.

With my hand on your chest
I'd ask you what was in there.
'My heart?' you'd reply.
'Far more,' I would deliver.

Your eyes would widen as I told you of the love
Placed there deep inside
But it didn't need to hide.

Love is good,
Love is kind,
Show it proudly,
Spread it widely.
Feel for people,
Show them grace
Regardless of their colour or race.

Buzz, your heart has grown to such a size,
Your emotions and feelings
You deliver with such pride
As they sway from side to side.
One minute you are happy,
Laughing at the world,
The next second you're wailing,
Your feelings derailing.

This can be confusing for us all,
Especially if your tears start to fall,
As your face creases up,
Your shoulders start to slump,

Before shaking with sadness
Or joy
Or gladness.

I know I look at you in disbelief,
Bewildered by the huge emotions
That have just erupted,
Like explosions.
But can I just say
I'm ever so proud
Of the love in your heart
That's been there from the start?

Letters on Motherhood

Love is good,
Love is kind,
Show it proudly,
Spread it widely.
Feel for people,
Show them grace
Regardless of their colour or race.

A QUICK SWITCH

Boys,

At the start of a long car journey you were all going berserk in the back. Buddy was copying all the baby sounds Max was making (mostly screeching and high-pitched squealing) and Buzz was moaning that it was too loud – making the whole scenario even louder. We had hours ahead of us and my brain was already scrambling for ideas on how we would get through the ride without us all being scarred at the end of it. I was in full-on patient-mum

mode, trying to find distractions and keep everyone in a good space (preferably your own space where you weren't winding each other up).

I reached for my phone to see what I could find, frantically searching my music library for something you'd all enjoy.

A new obsession had grown for Aerosmith simply because of the Rock 'n' Roller Coaster ride in Disney, which features the band and their music. Now, neither of you had actually been on it (you still haven't), but I think you were in awe of the ginormous guitar outside, which unsurprisingly captured your attention, thanks to your love of music and jumping around with guitars. We played you some of their songs but we quickly learnt that the music videos were a little frisky for innocent minds and instead we found ourselves at a video of someone on the actual ride.

You were sold. Aerosmith were cool.

So in an effort to keep us all entertained, I made a song and dance about listening to a really amazing track of theirs I'd found.

'I Don't Want To Miss A Thing' blasted through the speakers and you all just stopped what you were doing and listened. Even Max. The shift was instant, like a switch had been flicked in your minds.

As Steven Tyler's beautifully rocky voice filled the car, it felt like a miracle had occurred as we all sat in silence and just listened, appreciating the greatness of the epic song.

When it ended you asked to listen to it again – nicely. Even saying please.

We weren't even halfway through the second play when I turned around to find you all asleep. From manic craziness to zonked out in minutes. I have no idea how you *all* managed it. And in unison! You looked adorable.

We'd been banking on the motion sending you all

to sleep at some point in the journey, hoping your holiday siestas would help us along. Only not so early in the trip. My one concern was that it wasn't nap-time, only 11 a.m. I knew a nap then could potentially mess with the rest of the day. I toyed with the idea of waking you all up so that we could feed you and put you on the schedule I'd planned. A little anxiety tickled my brain over how emotional bedtime would be if Max had to spend an extra hour and a half awake – the early nap meaning he'd be awake from one-ish until 7 p.m., and what that might mean for the rest of the night . . . It's hard sticking to a baby's routine when you've got two other children in the mix, and it can be a stressful juggle to keep some sort of order and schedule while also allowing things just to happen and be more in the moment. Having said that, I used to be far more anxious about sticking to nap- and bedtimes when I only had Buzz and thought the world would end if we diverted from the plan at all. Third time lucky and I no longer had the luxury of ploughing all my energy into what one child was up to, and as a result I'd learnt that occasionally letting go could be brilliant.

The old adage *Don't look a gift horse in the mouth* sprang to mind.

The peace. The fact that everyone was content and calm in that precise moment. The unpredictability of what would happen if I decided to shake things up. It all stopped me doing anything other than lowering the volume of Aerosmith, and reaching across to grab your dad's hand.

Sometimes moments of calm have to be taken whenever they arrive.

Love you,
Mumma xx

Dear Fletcher boys,

I ran in my underwear across London today. Don't worry, I didn't just decide to strip off on a whim – it

was in aid of Celebrate You, a campaign that was part of the Vitality 10km, which saw over eight hundred women coming together and taking on the running challenge while stripped down to their basics. Showing that all of our bodies are wonderful, no matter our size or how much cellulite has decided to camp out on our thighs.

84

I'll admit that when I first got the email about it
from Bryony Gordon in February I initially said no.
Bryony, an incredibly inspiring journalist, author,
mental-health and body-positivity campaigner, is a
tough woman to say no to, but I thought it was a
marathon (she'd completed one the year before) and
knew I didn't have enough time to train and keep
my knees safe (they're a bit weak and rubbish).
When Bryony said it was only a 10k, I found myself
replying, 'Fuck it.' I told you she was a tough woman
to say no to.

Six weeks ago I started training. The first day
I went out I only ran for ten minutes – but I ran
continuously for those ten minutes. I didn't stop.
Afterwards I felt like I had a chest infection. My
breath had to fight so much to get down to my lungs,
and that sensation stayed with me for the whole of
that day. Regardless of how I felt afterwards, I was just
so happy that I'd kept running and not given up as
soon as my brain and legs told me to – that persistent
little voice telling me I could stop made itself heard
about twenty seconds in and continued for the
duration of my efforts.

The next run was another ten-minute one. It was
better. It didn't feel as hellish, and the wheezy chest

only stuck around for a short while after. It was the last time I felt that tightness in my throat. Since then I've gone from strength to strength – adding on a few minutes here and there, before today completing ten whole kilometres in one hour and fourteen minutes.

OK, so Mo Farah ran the same distance in twenty-eight minutes, but it really doesn't matter. It's not about beating an Olympian (good job, because most of us would fail before we'd even put our trainers on), it's about getting out there and doing it – and it's only been six weeks!

Six.

Isn't it amazing how quickly our bodies can adapt and get better at something when pushed? Who knows what else it can do that I've never given it the chance to experience through fear or lack of confidence in my own ability?

At the start of today I told myself it didn't matter what happened, whether I walked or ran it. The email chain from other women in our group reported injury after injury, with several people saying they were going to have to walk some, if not all, of the course. I'll admit, initially I was gutted as I got up to eight kilometres last weekend and felt ready to do the ten, but, more than anything, I just wanted to be a part of

the day and enjoy it. I told myself I could attempt a
10km at another time on my own, but today was about
more than us individually reaching our personal bests.
We had a message to share, which was that our shapes
and sizes are to be rejoiced in and celebrated, and that
exercise like running isn't exclusive to one body type.
We are all different, and that's a good thing. For too
long I've felt inferior to anyone thinner than me,
thought I was worth less because I didn't have a thigh
gap or a chiselled jaw. Well, those women's bodies can
be praised, but so can mine and every other body out
there. They're all pretty amazing. If you think about it,
we're all breathing miracles. How these collections of
cells come together and do what they do is beyond
me. It's magic.

It's taken me ages to begin to feel this way about
my body. I've directed so much negativity towards it
over the years – berated it for miscarrying, punished it
for taking up too much space, hated it for not looking
like I've been told it should look. But now I feel like a
total tit. Not only did my body grow three amazingly
wonderful boys and push them all out of my foof
(that's nature, boys), but it's still flipping standing and
enabling me to take on challenges like today's run,
and then the treks I do with CoppaFeel!.

I do not give it the credit it deserves.

Today I am in utter awe of it, and I hope the feeling of sheer elation as I crossed that finish line stays with me for ever. What a rush.

Wait!

I haven't talked about the underwear part yet! Well, I thought I'd feel self-conscious about stripping off

and running around London almost Nuddy Ned.
I didn't initially. I didn't really give it much thought,
but then as I started telling other people about the
challenge, the reaction they fired my way made me
feel like I should be embarrassed or nervous about
exposing what my mamma gave me. Yep, several
people I love and care about greeted my involvement
with frowns of confusion, a gawping mouth or words
that didn't say, 'You go, girl', more 'Really?' Each time
I was greeted with this reaction I just thought, Fuck!
and wondered what on earth I'd let myself in for, and
whether it was too late to back out without upsetting
anyone.

I won't lie, right up until two days ago I thought I'd
have to wear a top over my sports bra because I told
myself I couldn't possibly have my tummy out while
doing the run. It would jiggle around, my underwear
would ride up and roll down to expose more of my
rounded flesh. People would see too much of me, and
once those images were out there there'd be no way back
from it. The internet would keep them there for life!

I left the house this morning, my bag loaded
with a couple of extra top options and masses of
biodegradable body glitter. Would I cover up?
Or would I bring the party? I hadn't decided.

When your aunty Carrie and I arrived at the designated Celebrate You area we saw a string of photographers taking photos of Bryony and Jada Sezer, model, mental-health campaigner and, along with Bryony, the brainchild of the plan for us to run in our pants. Bryony and Jada were already in their underwear.

I did not feel nervous, just the usual apprehension at arriving somewhere new, settling in and saying hello to people.

My concerns lifted and dissipated immediately.

The sight of our leaders standing there with so much flesh on show, the world still spinning around them, people still going about their lives, felt so empowering. I decided not to wait for a mass de-robing moment when more runners joined us, and instead got out of my leggings and jumper without overthinking it. The air was a tad fresh, but a perfect running temperature. I reached into my bag and, instead of grabbing something to hide myself with, pulled out a pot of glitter and started sprinkling the contents on my face and body, laughing with my fellow runners as I handed it around and broke the ice. I didn't need to cover up. This was a celebration.

It's ironic that I let others have an impact on how

I felt about my body as I geared up to take part in a huge event about body confidence and positivity. It's not for others to decide how I view my own stretchmarks and cellulite. It's not for others to tell me what my body can and can't do. I might not look like a runner, but I've been training flipping hard – and I can now run further than those doubters could even though they're probably slimmer and might look fitter.

We've got to stop comparing and thinking one body type is preferable to any other but, more than that, we have to stop thinking we'll be judged, or should judge, for 'flaws' that are nothing but nature proving we're all perfectly unique and individual. For instance, when you've just grown a human you should not be in despair about what others might make of the skin that's stretched to help you work that magic. Your skin stretching was part of the wonder!

Earlier today you boys managed to catch sight of me running on the live stream coverage. When I got home you found it very funny that I was running down the street semi-naked.

Fair point.

Having been pregnant or nursing one of you relentlessly for the last five years, my body hasn't really felt my own. In many ways it has done and achieved

more than ever, but in terms of me physically doing
things like lifting and moving, it's got a little more
difficult. I've become my biggest size and my body
has ached and creaked more than ever. When I wake
up in the morning and shuffle to the loo or in to see
whoever has called me from my sleep, it takes a good
thirty seconds for my feet, hips and back to loosen
out of stiffness and become comfortable.

I used to feel really strong and never asked for your
dad's help with things like moving furniture, but now
I can't do the things I used to and feel weak. I don't
like that.

My training, today's run and the fact I will continue to run now that I've proved to myself that I can, has played a huge part in me finding my inner strength. I'm hoping that will build and give me all types of other strength too.

You three have been a huge catalyst for me wanting to get my body moving and to build my strength and fitness. Buzz and Buddy, you're only five and three years old, but so far you love being outside and going on adventures. Whether you're walking, running or cycling, you love a physical challenge. It dawned on me a little while ago that at some point, unless I improved my fitness, those adventures might not include all of us. I'd be the one left behind while you went and bonded in the wilderness.

No, thanks. I want to be exploring and having fun with you.

So, yes, Mumma ran in her underwear through the streets of London today, and that's the start of her getting ready to show you the world, before sitting back and letting you conquer it.

Love you,
Your Mumma xx

BACK WHEN YOU BECAME
A TRIPOD

Boys,

Towards the end of my pregnancy I had some routine
tests done because I'd mentioned to a midwife that
I'd had itchy hands. It was a hot summer and they
might just have been swollen. It had worn off
so I didn't think too much of it. The tests were

inconclusive, but because
my bile acids were higher
than the midwives' team
would've liked, I went
to see a specialist who
recommended I be
induced at thirty-nine
weeks if I hadn't gone
into spontaneous
labour by then.

As Buzz and Buddy were both born before that point the doctor felt I had a naturally shorter gestation period and there was no reason to keep the baby in there any longer. He would be safer out as the bile acid might mean I had intrahepatic cholestasis, a liver disorder that can develop in pregnancy and may lead to the baby arriving prematurely or stillborn. Needless to say, I welcomed the idea of being induced to prevent anything happening to the baby, and when Lizzie, one of the midwives, asked if I wanted a sweep at thirty-eight weeks I practically jumped on the bed. Using the hypnobirthing breathing I'd been practising, I took some deep breaths while she did her thing – in my head it wasn't too dissimilar to what I do with butter, rosemary and a turkey on Christmas Day. I digress, but just to say it wasn't as painful as I'd feared and only mildly uncomfortable.

Lizzie told us she had a high success rate with her sweeps and hoped we'd be back to see her on the labour ward within the next forty-eight hours.

Happy with that news, your dad and I went to the Riding House Café, one of our favourite lunch spots and had a nice, calm meal before heading home to Buzz and Buddy.

I went into frantic cleaning mode, spurred on by the subtle twinges I was experiencing that I hadn't been feeling earlier. I was making sure everything was tidied up and packing away the remaining toys when Buddy stood up on the armchair next to me.

Just as I said it was time to go up for a bath, out of the corner of my eye I saw Buddy's foot slip from the armchair and him flying forwards towards the coffee table, colliding with a horrifying bang.

I scooped him up quickly and held him tight, but I saw the dripping of blood and knew it was bad. Your dad ran in just as I was turning him over. We were both mortified to see the inch-long wound on his forehead that allowed us to see his skull.

Everything stood still as adrenalin kicked in.

Acting on impulse, we put a clean cloth on the wound and applied pressure, then grabbed both of you and put you in the car. Buddy, you were curled up in your dad's lap while I drove to the minor-injuries unit around the corner from our house. This was when we realized we'd forgotten money for parking and anything else the two of you might need if we were going to be sitting there a while. Your dad ran into the hospital with Buddy while I drove Buzz home to collect change and useful bits before hopping into the car again and whizzing back. We were gone for just five minutes, but Buddy had been ushered through immediately, with kind members of the public and staff realizing he was in a bad way and needed to be seen quickly.

We found Buddy on a bed, his wound cleaned up and exposed. It was like something you'd see in an old war film, like someone had shot him straight in the head.

The thing that struck me about this whole nightmare was Buddy's demeanour. He cried initially, but when he was lying back on that hospital bed he just observed the people around him, seemingly calm but intrigued. I'm guessing it was the shock, although Buddy also has a natural ability to shrug off the things most other children (including Buzz) would cry over.

Back out in the waiting room with a clean but open wound, Buddy lay with his head on my bump. I breathed him in, and the smell of his blood instantly transported me to your births. It was raw, metallic and sweet. My mind and my body went back to that place, and it was heartbreaking to see my little baby being so brave even though he must've been in so much pain and terrified.

It wasn't long before we were ushered back to a bed, and while we were waiting to see if Buddy was going to be pieced back together with steri-strips or if we were going to have to go to another hospital for stitches, I felt my first proper contraction. Yep! How's that for timing?

Knowing these things take a while, I kept my focus on Buddy as they steri-stripped his head, an appointment was made for the following day (which

I guessed I wouldn't be going to) with specialists at
another hospital, and then we were sent off.

Back at home, I put Buddy in our bed and stayed
with him. He didn't want to be left alone, and I didn't
want to leave him. I thought having a lie-down and
checking in with what was going on with my own
body would be a good thing. I needed to regain some
calmness and assess what was happening. A couple of
hours in and we called your grandparents over. I knew
I was in labour and would be heading to the hospital
that night – Buddy came so quickly that we had been

warned not to hang around. Therefore, it made sense
for them to be at ours and get some kip rather than
being woken in the middle of the night and having to
make the journey then.

I can remember walking around downstairs
and your nana and Ewad trying to have proper
conversations with me while I was having
contractions. I think I was trying to do everyday
stuff, like emptying the tumble-dryer, so it's hardly
surprising they were acting normally – they were
taking their cue from me.

They went up to bed and we phoned the hospital.
Everything was getting more intense, and we all
agreed that I was better off making my way in just in
case I ended up having the baby in the car on the A40.

OK, I flew through the other births. Buzz, I was
so zoned into my hypnobirthing practice that you
were basically breathed out, and, Buddy, you flew
out, but this baby wasn't sure how he wanted to
travel.

When I got to the hospital I was told I was between
one and two centimentres dilated. Not ideal as it
already felt quite intense, but the midwives were
amazing and I can remember lots of encouraging
smiles and peaceful chatting while I got on a bouncy

birthing ball, put on some hypnobirthing affirmations
and zoned out.

I remember being told in one of my appointments
that third babies can be a bit tricksy. It was a notion
that was repeated to me a few times by other people
in the know and I had managed to block it out

completely: I didn't think it was useful knowledge to
have . . . It would seem they were right in my case.
I was dilating very slowly, yet surges felt strong and
powerful. I got into the pool and just filled my head
with stuff I knew would make me feel happy and
calm – *The Comedy Roadshow* was streamed from
Netflix and I just went from breathing my way
through that to more affirmations.

Talking about breathing, I was twelve hours in
when I realized I'd completely forgotten how to
breathe – which is an integral part of the whole
hypnobirthing method. I can't tell you the difference
I felt within my body when I started sending breath
to all the places oxygen was needed. It was a
completely different experience, and I felt relaxed
and calm, rather than out of control and nervous.

Although I was most definitely focused on the
task in hand, my heart kept wandering to Buddy
and wondering what was going on with him at the
hospital. We'd tried to plan ahead in the hope the
baby would arrive during the night and your dad
would be able to nip out and be with Buddy, but
that was impossible. He couldn't miss the birth of
his child, and we knew Nana and Ewad would be
incredible with you. There was a strong sense of

guilt on my shoulders about not being there,
though, and I wouldn't be surprised if that played
a part in things taking longer than I'd expected.

I got stuck at six centimetres dilated for quite some
time. My waters still hadn't gone, and an examination
showed that the baby was stuck at a slightly funny
angle facing the side. Seeing as he'd been in that
position for the last ten weeks of my pregnancy
I knew he wasn't going to turn suddenly on his own. I
had to decide whether to keep going and risk myself
or the baby getting tired, or letting my experienced
midwife get involved. She was the same woman who
had helped deliver Buddy (but, like I said, he flew out)
and I trusted her judgement on what to do. We talked
a lot but ultimately I decided to let her break my
waters to help the baby out.

There was intense pressure straight away so
I got into the birthing pool, lay on my side with
my head out of the water, and zoned out with my
hypnobirthing. I'm not even joking when I say I fell
asleep. In active labour.

I felt an urge I recognized: the need to bear
down. I did as my body demanded and minutes
later I was flooded with oxytocin as I looked down
at our third son – Maxwell Mario Fletcher, born

on 24 August 2018, at 3.06 p.m., weighing exactly seven pounds.

Max, you've looked different from your brothers from day one, but still visibly one of them. You felt so new, but so familiar too.

All through my third pregnancy I'd felt I was expecting too much in thinking I could welcome a third healthy baby into the world – but there you were, nuzzling into me in the water. I felt so relieved and grateful.

I laughed, I cried, and I instantly fell in love.

Your aunty Giorgie was your first visitor, literally running across London so that she could meet you and steal some hugs.

I slept so well that night with you by my side . . . It was heavenly, and the last full night of sleep I remember having! I was zonked.

What a thrilling, unnerving and emotional way for four to become five.

What an adventure!

Mumma xx

IT'S NOT ME, IT'S YOU

Dear Phone,

You have been such a lifesaver for me: during the night feeds you have kept me company, kept me entertained and AWAKE! You've stopped me falling into a dangerous slumber that would've seen me passed out with a baby in my arms. Your various apps have kept my brain engaged and alert. From chuckling along to podcasts to Instagram scrolling, you've been there for me in the darkest hours when it seems the rest of the country is snoozing and no one is there to listen to my worries.

Thank you.

You've enabled me to carry on working anytime, anywhere. Received an email at softplay? No worries, you're on it. Have to post about a podcast episode but out in the park? No worries, you're on it. Need to jot a bit of inspiration down in Notes so I can expand on that thought later when the kids are asleep? No worries, you're on it.

Thank you . . .

You don't even wince when, let's be honest, I do a vast majority of admin on the loo – where I don't feel like I'm being a terrible mother for having you in my hand. Even though I try to keep the vast amount of our contact hidden, you do *not* make me feel guilty. You do *not* judge. You are just there.

Thank you.

You have connected me to so many people around the world. People who understand what I'm going through and have stopped me feeling so alone or ashamed of my failings as a mother. Social media gets a bad rep, but through you I have become part of an amazing community I learn so much from. You have helped build my confidence and taught me to trust my own intuition and instincts.

Thank you . . .

Although, thinking about it, a friend of mine recently left social media entirely, his reason being that he found he spent more time looking at other people's children than his own. When you follow other mums and dads online, who proudly share pics of their children, and then find yourself mindlessly scrolling, that's a fair point. I can understand where he was coming from.

Hmm . . .

Maybe now is a good time to talk to you about my own concerns.

There's no nice way to tell you this, but recently you've been putting me on edge. Your presence makes me feel anxious. Perhaps it's because Max will be a year old in a couple of months and I know I'll have to get fully immersed in my work again when that happens. I've juggled work and looking after him at home thus far (he's been the best sleeper of the three and I can get a lot done in his two-hour nap, plus Tom has been here to tag team when Buzz and Buddy are at school) but I know work is building for the second half of the year and that this 'loose' maternity leave will need to

turn into something more structured, my mother-in-law taking care of Max in the days while I write.

I know, because you keep reminding me.

You sit there, calling me, telling me I have to respond to something or be somewhere. I've started to feel like you might be robbing me of time I won't get back. I feel like you're encroaching on something that should never have been yours. Even if it's not work-related, you suck me in with a feed I lovingly curated, the news or messages or calls from others I know and love . . .

I know, I know.

You give me so much: how could I possibly be thinking negatively of you? But things have become complicated between us.

In fact . . .

You're always on silent.

Did you know that?

That's why I don't respond instantly to your alerts.

And I've started turning you face down.

That way I can't see you glowing at me with demands.

And I've turned off most notifications.

I'm not going through my day with a wave of *likes* giving me validation for existing but actually living my day with the people I truly care about more than anything.

I've been slowly disengaging.

Dare I say it, sometimes I *like* leaving you behind. I *like* having some distance between us, even if we're just in separate rooms or, better yet, on separate floors. I'd never leave home without you – I'm not foolish. You're my beacon of safety, after all. But around the house, when I'm with the kids, it's different.

For a long time our relationship has been on your terms, but it's time for me to regain control and tell you to back off.

I'm not breaking up with you, it's not a divorce, but I do need some space. A bit of separation so that you don't come to mean more to me than you should.

I want to come to you on my terms. Scroll, then go, feeling empowered, informed and fab.

I want to play with my children and not feel a pull to check if you have anything to share with me every two minutes. I want to bury myself in motherhood and not feel torn.

Times have changed.

While I value all you have to offer, and will continue to use your services, it will be at a diminished rate, at dedicated times. On my terms.

And don't try coming at me with some new app that's been created to get my brain fired up and addicted.

Nope.

No, thanks.

The honeymoon period is over.

I love you, but I don't always like you.

Yours (sometimes),
Giovanna

PS I hate to say it but loo-based admin will be remaining 'a thing'. Sorry, but that is definitely a habit I can't shake and it's very productive. Using those three minutes to clear my inbox gives me *such* clarity!

BEDTIME CHATTER

We're currently having a tug of war at bedtime with you both wanting one of us to stay while you fall asleep, even though you share a room and have each other for company. The only problem is that Buddy wants me and, Buzz, you want your dad.

Tonight was my turn to stay.

Buzz: I want Daddy to stay. He's the bestest daddy in the world ever and he plays Lego with me.

Me: Buzz, you have me tonight. (*Said in my best firm but fair and loving voice, while holding back a chuckle at how cute you are.*)

Buzz: I want Daddy. (*You actually wail as though he's left us, rather than gone to the loo.*)

Me: But aren't I the bestest mummy? (*Keeping it playful.*)

Buzz: No! (*Firm. Adamant!*)

Me: Who is? (*Keeping it light. Keeping it cheerful – trying to see the funny side even though my heart is already bruising.*)

Buzz: Aunty Giorgie.

Me: I see . . . Night then, Buzz. Love you.

I sit on the floor and text the bestest mummy in the world. She tells me my niece, Summer Rae, had called her 'nasty' that afternoon because Giorgie stopped her shaking shredded paper everywhere 'like snow'. Buzz's words became an odd comfort to her.
    Kids.

Dear Fanny,

Can you believe you brought me three gorgeous boys?
I mean, you didn't grow them, but you were the
tunnel from their first home and into my arms.

Three kids.
That's a lot of traffic.
That's a lot of give.
That's a lot.
I'll stop.
I have changed as a person thanks
to my life experiences, and you,
too, have changed because of what
you've experienced. Change is
expected. Change can be glorious.
Change can be fine. Change *is*
different.

I hate the phrase 'like watching your favourite pub burn down' in relation to you being a part of birthing babies. It makes me angry that the monumental involvement you have with delivering life is belittled by being compared to an overcrowded room, with sticky floorboards and stinky toilets next door. Let's not forget how damaging words can be, and how fragile they can make someone who is already vulnerable feel. Pushing a baby out is no small feat, and adding to the anxiety of what might happen beforehand, then making someone feel overly self-conscious afterwards about what has happened 'down there' is inconsiderate, crass and immature.

Is it really a laughing matter?

Funny how that particular joke is made by men, not women who have had their 'bits' altered through childbirth.

What some twerp has deemed 'bantz' down a pub is something many have to live with, then feel shame and humiliation for. Getting *you* out and putting you on display shouldn't feel like an act of bravery, should it?

I studied you. After each baby arriving I got a handheld mirror and studied you. I mean, not straight away – you were pretty impossible to see over the

empty baby pouch, and I was scared after Buzz
because I'd had stitches and couldn't move. I thought
I was being a wimp, but it turned out you were
infected. A loose stitch. I was asked if I wanted the
stitch put back in. No, thanks. It was horrible to think
of anyone else tinkering with you when you were
already going through such trauma.

Trauma. We don't use that word when thinking
about you and your efforts in childbirth, but there's
no denying you get hit with quite a bit of it as you're
stretched to your limits and, in my case, sometimes
beyond. Actually, you were cut. As I lay there on the
bed pushing my baby out I was told an episiotomy
was necessary. I really didn't want one, and was
advised in hypnobirthing to stick to my guns on
that, but I wanted my baby to get out safely. In that
moment I might've moaned at the thought of having
a scalpel placed anywhere near you, but there was
no way I'd go against what I was being advised by a
medical professional, who was there to protect me
and my baby. He knew things I didn't, so in he went
with his blade.

I cannot remember how that felt, though I'm pretty
sure I was given an injection to numb the area before
you were sliced.

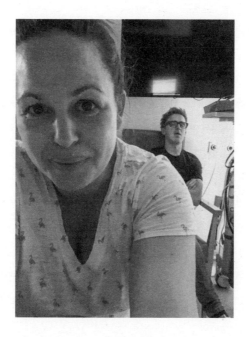

My memory might be patchy, but I do remember how you felt afterwards when you'd been threaded back together – a startled and sore patchwork fanny. I remember how I would have to cup you, my hand covered with loo roll, when going for a poo in case the stitches holding you together (not the loose one, obviously) pulled apart and left you more exposed than you ought to be. I remember how cupping you eased the pressure and discomfort. How when I walked I'd have to stop and catch my breath, as though part of you had been caught – like a thread on a jumper being snagged.

I'm wincing as I write this, yet, interestingly, I've not crossed my legs to protect you like I normally do when hearing others talk on the subject. Maybe that's because this letter is for you, and it would be hypocritical to protect you now when I couldn't before.

Too profound? Maybe.

I was scared of looking at you that first time. Frightened of what I might see. You were in excruciating pain, tender and swollen, so I knew you'd be different. I caught a glimpse of you. Stitches are never pretty, are they? They always conjure up images of Frankenstein, no matter where they are on a body. Plus, you were badly bruised. Black and blue.

Ooft.

You know when someone is beaten up and you see the before and after pictures in the paper? Well, that was you. Yet as the bruises faded and cuts healed, I waited to see what we were left with. It's been the same each time. And I've felt a twinge of sadness as I've watched you recover. I mean, obviously you've done your best each time, but you've had a fair deal to mend from. You were never going to ping back entirely, and I don't want you to feel bad about that. You have not let me down, it's just that I needed time to process these changes, no matter how big or small.

Oh, my!

I've just remembered that after the first delivery you couldn't pee straight. Wee would veer to one side, streaming across my right thigh, the result being that I always ended up with urine where it shouldn't be. I couldn't stop the stream going where it wanted to. I never talked about it to anyone and just tried to accept it as something embarrassing I was going to have to live with, shamefully, for the rest of my life. Strangely, my second delivery seemed to cure my wonky peeing. It was an instant fix and I thanked the midwife at my six-week check in case it was down to her delicate stitching skills.

Oh, yes, you did get stitched second time round too, but this time you'd torn. Not massively, but enough to require being sewn back together. It sounds horrific, I know, but I think we'd both agree that that worked out better for us both. Less painful, easier to heal from – and it resulted in me not having to wee all over myself every loo trip.

Thankfully, the third stay in the hospital didn't change things back, although I did spend a long time wondering if I'd suffered a prolapse – seriously, things were hanging down where they should not have been. Three weeks in I even had to end a walk

early because I was worried I was going to lose an organ . . . I had to shuffle as slowly as I could out of the park and back to the car. There was just a heaviness down there.

Oh, Fanny.

You are harder to declare acceptance of and talk about than the wobble on my tummy and stretch marks on my thighs, possibly because you never made me feel sexy to start with – which is strange when you're my sexual organ. You're an odd part of the female body that's always hidden. You and your lot, you're all funny-looking . . . and now you're even weirder. Plus, and this is something I'm quite irked with you for doing, in the life after birth-giving, you've started to collect my rare (silent) bum trumps and seem to like regurgitating them in a rather embarrassing fashion. Why, Fanny? Why? Although Caitlin Moran confessed to me on the podcast that hers collects bathwater, which whooshes out five minutes later – seems birth makes you all a bit grabby!

You are quite the complex mistress and I couldn't write a series of letters on motherhood without addressing one to you because your changes are directly linked to me becoming a mum. Trying to accept your new lumps and bumps while navigating my way through my new role as a mother have run parallel. We went through something monumental together and have been trying to make sense of it ever since.

I've come to realize that there's no point in looking

back to what once was because, unless I want a designer vagina (not the route for me, ta), you are the one I've got. I have to learn your new ways and adapt. I have to break down my hang-ups, find some fanny positivity chatter on Instagram (I'm blooming certain there'll be some) and get on with our lives.

I'm sorry I've spent so long being wary and ashamed of you.

Oh, and if the twats down the pub are right, thanks for sacrificing your sticky floorboards to deliver me so much.

Yours for ever,
Her upstairs xxx

A WASTE OF TIME?

Dear Buddy,

I have just spent fifty minutes in the garden scrubbing your mud kitchen. It is meant to be for mud (der!), leaves, twigs and other things you might find in the outside world. However, the other day I found some out-of-date ginger and thought you'd enjoy sprinkling it on top of your collected pile of dirt. This led to you having a little bit from a few of the jars of ingredients in the cupboard, then escalated to you having a full bag of out-of-date flour. As you can imagine, this caused quite a mess. You were so impressed with yourself, though, as you took our food orders and got down to baking, boiling, pouring and stirring. You chattered away to yourself, your eyebrows knitted together in concentration as you went about your tasks. At some point you decided the flour was worthy of more than just sieving between pots and cups, and decided to pretend it was sand. You lay down and poured the lot over your tummy, as though you were playing on a beach.

You laughed so much.

Next the hose was on. You were washing yourself down (sort of) and adding water to bowls and swishing things around, so everything got a little sloppy.

You went to bed a happy and exhausted little boy tonight. It was only when I went outside to tidy up that I noticed just how much mess had been created, but I didn't care. I didn't spend today saying no, and you didn't test your boundaries or act out. Today with you was effortless, and I feel I need to revel in the success.

Seeing you lost in your own little world, using your imagination and dreaming up a scenario was worth the time I spent tidying up, because I know being a three-year-old is hard. I know being the second child is challenging. I know it's frustrating having feelings you can't communicate. I know it's tough when the world places so much expectation on how you should behave and express yourself.

Today you were free.

I love you,
Mumma xx

Dear Mum,

It's fair to say the two of us have brought children up in very different times. We had a conversation today about what it was like for you. You didn't drive then (you'd had an accident that scared you away from doing so for many years), so we got the bus everywhere. That's three kids, under five, on buses . . .

As I'm writing this, I have three children under five and I have no idea how you did it. Obviously I've taken the three boys out to other people's houses on my own, but if Tom is away working and I'm home alone with the kids, I'd

126

rather go for an adventure through the field at the back of our house than take them to the park where people might judge us if they play up. I also worry I might lose one of them and reason that there's little chance of that in a big open field with no one around.

I can't imagine the stress you would've gone through, trying to get us all to sit nicely on the bus without hitting each other, to stop squabbling over nothing, or to follow you around the shops without running off and getting lost.

I remember those trips to Romford or Ilford. If we misbehaved, you'd hiss a warning at us, your eyes flaring with anger and sternness, telling us that if we carried on you'd take us home . . . and you always kept your word, no matter what we were doing. On one occasion when we were playing up on our way to somewhere fun (probably giddy and excited, or simply winding each other up because that's something we've always been very good at), you told us that we would go home if we carried on. Sure enough, as soon as we arrived at our destination you made us turn around and go home. Literally we got off one bus and then got straight on the other going in the opposite direction. I wonder if we cried and wailed an apology

or just took it on the chin and understood that it was our own fault.

Did you almost give in and change your mind? Did you want to let us have fun since you'd gone through the effort of getting us there? Or were you too annoyed to back down and think that if you did we'd never learn the difference between right and wrong?

With three kids you had to put your foot down to be taken seriously. Your actions let us know you weren't to be messed with, and we knew to listen . . . most of the time.

In an HMHB podcast episode Liz Earle talked about how children have lots of friends and only one mother, so we should take that role seriously and understand that we won't always be liked. It's not easy, though, is it, Mum? It's difficult having little faces looking up at you with such sadness, and sometimes anger, and knowing you could make it all better by giving them whatever they want – even though they've been naughty.

I always felt sorry for the kids who were shouted at in public or, God forbid, got smacked. At least you only gave us the eyes (a look I'm yet to master with the boys but am trying to perfect) or a stern hiss. You would always hold it together when we were at other people's houses, but as soon as we were in the car you could guarantee a debrief of our behaviour. On another occasion, after we'd been to see family friends Anna and Horace, you did your most famous appraisal – one we pull out of the memory bank and remind you of at most family get-togethers. The one that makes you blush.

You started clapping from the passenger seat. Slowly.

Sarcasm dripping with every beat.

'Well done, kids. Ten out of ten. We won't be going there again.'

We sat aghast in the back of the car. Usually you let things build and then we'd get a 'good' smack or, if you were really angry, a slipper thrown across the room – you had surprisingly good aim when we were your target. That particular tactic was new, and it scared the crap out of us. At least we knew where we stood with the shouting. The calm approach was more fear-inducing than previous attempts to control us, and the shame of our behaviour came flooding in. I know we rib you for that day but it's stuck with me because, rather than thinking about a prickly slapped bottom or wiping away snivelling tears, it caused us all to sit and ponder our behaviour.

Mum – you cracked parenting that day!

Today is the first time I've heard you talk about how you used to feel when we acted out. You used the word 'humiliated', although I could tell you were uncomfortable saying it because you know how big that word is to pin on children – but I get it. I've recently read a book about triggers, and how when our children misbehave we are triggered to react in a certain way, according to how we were brought up. Today you used a phrase I've never heard before in parenting, but it was true of your generation growing up, and how you were taught to discipline: 'Hit first, ask questions later.' There were six of you and your siblings in one house, so I imagine the fastest way to shut you all up in a drama was to give you a 'clip around the ear' or 'a good hiding', then get to the root of what was going on once everyone was scared into submission. So, as an adult, when your children weren't acting in a way your parents would've approved of – maybe we were being too loud, arguing, fighting or being just plain difficult – I can understand that you would feel lost on how to respond and then ashamed. I know that feeling, because I have days when I feel like I have zero control over the boys. See? The frustration and rage have been passed on, and although I do try to suppress the narky bitch and tell her she's barking up the wrong tree by shouting, I know she's there, itching to get out and explode in what feels like a quick fix.

But it's not a fix. If anything, it just causes the situation to escalate further and truly erupt.

It's something that's played on my mind a lot since

Arlene Phillips and her daughter Alana Stewart were on the podcast – these chats have become like therapy, Mum. A way to understand us all a little better. Well, having just become a grandma for the first time, Arlene found herself looking back and reflecting on how she mothered and how, like many, she would lose her temper. It made me wonder what I'll look back on and regret. Now, Shouty Mum hasn't made an appearance for months, but I know there are still situations I don't handle in the best way and regret instantly. Did I say something with too much venom? Did I fail to listen to what was being said? Should I have tried a different tack sooner? Have I made my children scared of me? Will they close off and disengage? Will they stop loving me because I've been too firm and haven't given in? Do they realize they are my absolute world and that I'd do anything for them?

I think as mums we're conditioned to doubt our choices and wonder what we could've done better – and that is because we care. Children are meant to test their boundaries, explore and experiment. They need time to understand and grasp what is expected of them. As a direct result, we can feel we're losing control of them – but maybe we're meant to!

The world is a baffling place, and as children discover how to cope with their needs and desires, how to handle not getting the things they want and how to behave, they will make 'mistakes'. Those mistakes cause mums like you and me – who want them to behave so that others know what delightful kids they can be – feel lost.

Perhaps the more we speak about those emotions the less alone we will feel, and the more we'll understand ourselves and adapt our methods. Earlier you told me you know exactly when you last smacked one of us, and when you decided to make a change. I'm currently going through the same thing with my shouting. I, like you, don't want my children to be scared of me. Instead I want their respect, so I'm trying my best to react in a calmer fashion and put their emotions before my own. On the whole it's working and, weirdly, has enabled me to deal with the situations in a much more measured way . . . It still surprises me when they actually listen, although it doesn't always work and at times I have felt a bit pathetic. I'll get there!

I'm sorry you occasionally (because there were ruddy good times too – loads of them) had such a terrible time mothering us. And I'd like to say sorry for being such a nightmare child. It might surprise people to know that I was the monkey of the family (especially when I had glue ear) – but, more than that, I'm sorry you weren't given the support and encouragement you needed to help you manage us.

Another podcast guest during a live show explained that her mum had always tried to be her best friend but what she really wanted was a mother. Her words really landed with me. You and I have

never been in a mother–daughter relationship where
I call you five times a day or the pair of us hang out
all the time. I love you unconditionally, but we are
not two peas in a pod (although Tom is forever
saying I'm like you). We've not been besties, and
you've never interfered with anything going on in
my life. Instead you've been my mother. For that
you will always be the one I turn to when I really
need comfort or support, and I know you will always
be the one to put me back together when the chips are
down. I know that whenever I need you you're there
without question. You would drop anything for your
children and we're all so grateful for that. We grew up
in a house where we knew how to behave and that
there'd be consequences if we were naughty, but
ultimately we were a tight-knit family who put each
other first.

I feel so very lucky to have been brought up
under your roof. You were my first female role
model, and there's no doubt I am who I am because
of you and the environment you made for us at
home. I didn't feel comfortable being me out of
the house, but within our walls I could flourish.
Thank you for allowing me to make mistakes,
learn and grow!

You asked me recently if I thought you were a good mum. The vulnerability broke my heart. Not only did it make me realize I will be continuously asking myself the same question, but it also made me wonder if I've let you know how special you are, enough. Mum you gave us your all. There is no one else I'd rather have as my number one. You're more than a good mum, and I'm lucky to call you mine.

I will love you always,
Giovanna xx

Dear Boys,

There have been times when I felt I'd lost each of you.
Times when you've been difficult, times when you've
asked for your dad over me,
times when I've felt I've been
punished for being absent, being
firm, or for focusing on one
of your siblings.

Yet . . .

You always find your way back.

But each time I wonder if I've
pushed you too far, and
disappointed you more than you can
handle.

Tonight Buddy wanted Daddy to
put him to bed, not me. I tried not to

take the rejection to heart. But now, five hours later, as Buddy is lying in bed next to me, draping his arms over my shoulders, staking a claim to his spot on my pillow after telling me he loves me, I'm reminded of this push and pull, and how naturally it happens in most households.

I love you all so much. You can push me away all you like. I just have to remember to breathe you in a little deeper each time you return with a pull.

Mumma xxx

WHAT IS SUCCESS?

Dear Boys,

I was with my drama school friends this weekend –
the brilliant bunch I met at Rose Bruford back in
2003. Only a couple are still acting. Most, like me,
have found themselves using the skills they
accumulated in other ways, like teaching, or in
production – one has even set up his own company
for children's parties called Froggle, which he's about
to take to New York!

It's fair to say most of us aren't doing what we
thought we would be when we left drama school for
the last time in 2006, and this weekend we shared an
interesting conversation about success.

If we look at our lives in black and white then the
majority of us have already failed. We are not big
Hollywood actors, or prancing on the West End stage

or becoming new regulars on *EastEnders* or *Corrie* –
those were things we thought we would be doing. Or
at least we thought they were nearer to our grasp than
they actually were. Our lives took other routes while
we navigated our way through the realities of being an
out-of-work/jobbing actor. We had to put those
dreams on hold while we explored our creative juices
in different ways, obtained financial stability elsewhere,
and found other ventures that made us happy.

We've failed, but that has not made us failures because
we have succeeded in many different ways and have been
able to adapt. We could have stuck at it, got ourselves
hooked on a dream that simply wasn't going to come
true – yet that might have cost us too much mentally,
emotionally and physically. It's hard to know whether
'giving up' took more courage and guts than just sticking
it out and being miserable, but not one of my friends
looked fraught over that decision this weekend.

In our varying job roles, and in our home lives,
we'll fail and succeed every day. Some of us will spend
years chasing a huge life-long dream, then celebrate it
finally coming true, while others will take pride,
happiness and contentment in something surprising
that they've been able to open their heart to – who is
anyone to say that's not a success?

At school my friends were always going for auditions or getting acting jobs when I wasn't. I always felt I was failing before I even got through the door. These days, I think that if I hadn't had those experiences my life would look very different from what it is. There have been relationships that have failed, friendships that have fallen apart, but in a roundabout way those failings have pushed me towards people for whom I have a mutual respect and love.

Even my daily successes and failures build up and have an impact on my mind. To me, getting to meetings early, rather than on time, is success. Getting there late is a huge fail as it makes me feel rude to those I'm meeting. In a fail of a writing day I can find myself in a really negative headspace where I question everything, yet on a successful one, work feels so effortless. Going to bed early and getting a good night's sleep – huge success. Being unable to settle because of intrusive thoughts – massive fail.

What is important is realizing the things you're doing well and giving yourself a pat on the back. It's great to have a goal and something to work towards, but sometimes we can be so busy looking at what other people are doing, or fretting about where we think we should be in our lives, that we forget to look at all the things we've achieved, how far we've come on our journey and how we're boshing life in our own unique way.

I see this so much in motherhood, where it's possible to get to the end of the day and feel you've failed because there were about a dozen meltdowns, because no one ate the dinner you'd spent ages making or because you shouted just before bedtime . . . I know this because it happens to me so often. Motherhood is the biggest illusion of failure. We feel the weight of those 'failures' so hugely because

we care so much and love so keenly . . . That looks like success to me!

Do not be put off or sucked in by the words SUCCESS and FAILURE. Just live your life and give it your all, while allowing yourself to alter your path, follow your heart and take on new challenges. That way, whatever the outcome, you've succeeded in spirit, love and dedication.

Pep-talk done.

Mumma xx

MOVIE PERFECT TURNED REALITY

Dear Buddy,

Tonight, in a picturesque moment as I lay next to you and did my best to breathe in all your loveliness, I put my forehead to yours and whispered, 'I love you.' You softened into me further, clearly comforted by the motherly love that was oozing into you.

'Mumma?' your little voice squeaked.

'Yes,' I replied, my voice soft, loving, and like something from a Hollywood movie: the music underneath would be delicate and romantic, the camera shot an extreme close-up, perfectly capturing our mushy nuzzling.

You paused and turned your head to look at me, your big brown eyes taking me in with a contemplative expression on your face. You are blooming gorgeous.

'Yes, Bubba?' I prodded with a smile.

'You're a poohead,' you stated, before turning and pulling my arm tighter around you so that we formed the perfect pair of spoons.

And that's our current reality . . . and I wouldn't have it any other way.

Love, your poohead
Mumma xx

Dear Buzz,

At parents' evening a couple of months ago your
reception-class teacher told us that you have 'a joy
and enthusiasm for life'. Oh, my heart was set
to burst.

Never lose that.

What a talent.

What a treasure.

Then last week you won a school award for your
reading. I actually gasped when your name was called
out, but I shouldn't have been surprised. You love
reading and will try to read any word you come across.
This has led us into a few interesting chats, like when
you read a poster in the women's toilets about periods.
Overall, however, it's amazing to see your brain take a
word and try to figure it out, and sometimes just spin

off a sentence without any hesitation. It's nothing short of pure magic!

Knowing that you're happy, intrigued and bouncing your way through your schooldays makes me incredibly proud. You are bright with a thirst for knowledge, and I hope we'll always be able to facilitate that passion rather than force you into studying or chasing after a particular job.

It's not the same for everyone. Last year I was chatting to a fellow parent at a party. He was telling me how his son went to a different school from yours because he needed to be pushed 'so that he can become a doctor or a lawyer'. He needed that extra nudge. The dad then went on to say that his daughter didn't need the same approach because the school you're currently at would nurture her and help her to become 'a good friend, a good wife, a good mother'. I think my jaw hit the floor. I was speechless and don't think I replied at all. You cannot debate someone else's decisions for their child, or their view of them, while trying to hand out chicken nuggets to hungry four-year-olds.

The sexist comment aside, I do understand the desire of well-meaning parents to help their children get the best start in life, especially if they've had to struggle themselves, but what is the cost?

Part of me wonders whether I'm doing you a disservice by not doing the same, but then I remember. You are five years old. In my opinion pressure and childhood should never be mixed: you have a lifetime of angst ahead of you but you'll only ever have one childhood. I really do think you have to spend that wisely. These are your carefree days. Enjoy them.

I hope we manage to help you and your brothers become the best version of yourselves, and that you enjoy the whole of your life rather than frantically feeling you're always on the way somewhere or to becoming something. You don't have to keep pushing

and hoping to please other people. Sometimes stopping and being 'good' is just as beneficial to you and those around you. Being 'good' and showing compassion, love and kindness to those you meet along the way is what life is about. Sod doing things for us!

Boys, I want you to carry on soaking up the world at your own pace, and I look forward to watching you do so with pride.

Love you,
Mumma xx

Dear Boys,

We're currently three weeks into the summer holidays and things have not gone as planned. We were all

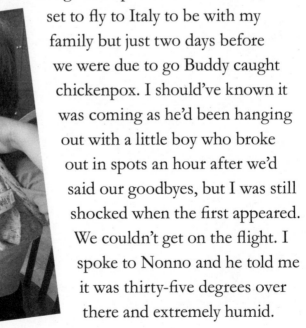

set to fly to Italy to be with my family but just two days before we were due to go Buddy caught chickenpox. I should've known it was coming as he'd been hanging out with a little boy who broke out in spots an hour after we'd said our goodbyes, but I was still shocked when the first appeared. We couldn't get on the flight. I spoke to Nonno and he told me it was thirty-five degrees over there and extremely humid.

The heat would probably have added to the itchiness.
And if we had got there (we probably could've hidden
the spots because they were mostly on your body),
chances were Buzz or Max would've caught it and
then we wouldn't have been allowed to fly back . . .
Plus, I hated the thought of a stranger getting ill by us
taking that risk.

So, I made the decision to keep us at home,
cancelled our seats on the plane, and declared it as
one of those things. (We did get our money back in
the form of easyJet vouchers so it wasn't all bad!)

We stayed at home, got out the paddling pool,
bought a trampoline, used the boxes it came in to

make a den in the bushes, and tried our best to find ways to keep you all entertained and stop you hitting each other.

It was tough but we made it through.

We even had fun.

This was mostly because Buddy had quite a mild case of the illness and was still able to live his normal 'Buddy ways'. Buddy, you practically shrugged the whole thing off and were as nutty as ever. You didn't stop from the moment you got up in the morning, and were just as enthused, bash-full (not bashful, definitely not that – rather, continuously bashing your brothers) and courageous as ever. You got on with it and wouldn't slow down to be poorly.

We've always known that as soon as one of you was struck with it the other two would be sure to follow. We'd had it easy with Buddy, and we knew it. It was a long two-week wait and I started to doubt that you'd all get it in the same time period, even though I'd had dozens of inbox messages warnings of the two-week interlude and how transference between siblings increases the severity of the symptoms.

Then, three days before we were due to drive to Cornwall, still hopeful we'd make it on a family holiday of some kind, it happened. Buzz, you were the next man down and it hit you hard. You have been very, very, very poorly. You have been covered with spots from head to toe and have had a very high fever. You've writhed around in your sleep while in our bed, been as pale as a sheet and off your food.

My instant thought was to cancel Cornwall too, but then I remembered we'd be travelling in the car and staying in our own little house. Once there, we could get you better and then you'd still be able to enjoy time on the beach.

I can't tell you how awful I felt on the drive down when I turned around to see you sitting between your brothers in the back of the car, looking awful. I felt like I was being transported to the future and seeing what you were going to look like as a teenager hitting puberty – tall and skinny, with dozens of spots on your face. It didn't help that I'd put the chickenpox cooling foam through the front of your hair, making it appear lank and greasy.

You looked so miserable, and I seriously doubted my decision to travel with you during that journey – especially when Buddy kept winding you up by chucking his own leg over his car seat so that his foot was hovering in front of your face. Brothers!

Anyway, we got here and you were brilliant. You

didn't moan at all on that first night when Dadda took Buddy to the beach for an hour while I cooked dinner. You chilled out on the sofa, playing with your toys and watching TV, happy to just space out a little.

That night you ate some dinner and your skin didn't seem to irritate you quite as much as it had the day before. When you went on to have a full night of uninterrupted sleep I was relieved that we'd gone along with our plans, satisfied that you'd get better and would be able to join in with the fun in no time.

The next morning, though, our first morning in Cornwall, we woke up and discovered Max had sprouted spots overnight – his body didn't want to wait the much-discussed two weeks and had jumped the gun. This left us with one child who could now be welcomed back into civilization (even though he looked a little scary), one who was desperate to get out and hit the beach, and a baby who was in good spirits but now confined to the house.

Ah, bugger.

On the first day the spots didn't seem too bad, Max, leading us to wonder if you had a mild case, like Buddy – perhaps thanks to still being breastfed and

gaining a little immunity. However, the next day that
theory was thrown off a nearby cliff as more spots
appeared and the ones on your face looked painful
and angry – it was more like hand, foot and mouth
disease, although it clearly wasn't. You were not a
happy boy, but could be tempted into smiling at
certain points of the day. You loved an oat bath, and
every time you had one you'd grab the sock of oats
and give it a suck, then screw up your face in
disgust. You had about ten of the baths (I lost a lot of
socks) and each time you couldn't resist taking it to
your mouth. Your appetite was also affected, largely

thanks to the massive ulcer at the front of your tongue. You were selective but happy to eat banana, mango, cheese and white bread. We just let you get on with it, satisfied that you managed to eat, unlike Buzz, whose ribs are on show after three days of starving.

The nights have been terrible. Every movement has woken you up. My instant reaction has been to pick you up and feed you to provide some comfort, in the hope it'll help you drift off. It hasn't always worked – and when it has you've been up an hour later . . . My boobs are going to hate me when you start sleeping again!

Seeing as the beaches are so huge down here, when the tide is out I've taken you down to the beach for an hour or two in the afternoons. We've managed to stay away from other people completely so that we didn't spread the gift of the clucking pox – we just felt the sea air would do you some good. It's not been too hot, there's been a nice cool breeze, and you've enjoyed playing in the sand and having a crawl around. It's given you a little freedom, and I think that's perked you up a bit each day.

Three consecutive run-ins with chickenpox have taught me that days two, three and four are the worst. Each time I was lulled into a false sense of

security with how calm the spots appeared on day one, and how few of them there were. But it's when they start blistering and making themselves truly known that the real fun begins.

In hindsight, this summer was probably the best opportunity for you all to get poorly as your dad and I had time blocked out in our diaries anyway. At least being off has meant I've not had to worry about cancelling work, or feeling wrenched about leaving you if the job has been too big to get out of. I've not had to let anyone down, which has eliminated any mum-guilt that probably would've occurred at another time. Silver lining in the cloud.

Thank heavens for Cornwall, giving us a beautiful backdrop to recover. Even though this trip will be linked for ever to oat baths, blisters and scabs, it has still managed to provide us all with happy memories of early-morning beach strolls, creeping into caves to look for monsters, and splashing around in warm tide pools in the late afternoon. Roll on next year when we can explore it even more!

Last night, Max, you had a big bowl of pasta and today you can't stop grinning . . . I think we've done it, boys! We've conquered chickenpox and it's turned into one area of childhood your dad and I can relax about, one we can tick off the long list! Well done!

Love you,
Mumma xxx

POX DELIGHT

Buzz,

You're starting to get a real sense of humour and you
frequently make me cackle! I love seeing the delight
on your face and the way your eyes sparkle when your
jokes land. I mean, it's been a long time coming. Your
'jokes' and understanding of them has been a ropy
experience, but now you're getting there and it's
delightful.

Chickenpox hit you hard. You had some serious
fevers and would be in terrible pain at night. Even in
your sleep you'd be moaning and writhing around.
Around 10 p.m. one night you wandered down the
stairs looking a complete state. We stopped what we
were doing and snuggled up on the sofa, talking about
things that made you happy, managing to perk you up.

In a moment of silence you clucked.

Literally clucked.

Your chickenpox was taking over.

You were turning full-on chicken.

We cracked up, and you joined in, happy that we understood. Thus making the whole thing funnier.

You're smart!

Mumma xx

TIMING IS EVERYTHING

Dear little loves of mine,

This morning it all felt a bit much, the screaming, the shouting, your inability to just leave one another alone and the constant need to be hitting or prodding each other . . . which resulted in me getting bashed when I tried to be the referee. It was intense and I felt like I was in an episode of *Supernanny*. I was sure Jo Frost was going to walk in any second, look on disapprovingly at your inappropriate behaviour and let me know where I was going wrong.

If I'd had a moment to start this letter then, it would have opened 'I've fucked this parenting thing up'.

I couldn't figure out where I was going wrong and why so often I felt out of my depth.

Fast-forward to an hour later when Buzz is playing nicely with his Marvel heroes, Max is napping and Buddy's being charmingly delightful, chuckling away as we put hands and feet in paint. I'm reassured that I'm actually doing an all-right job after all.

Parenting is a constantly moving thing. Sometimes it all seems too much and other times I feel like my heart could burst with the love, pride and joy that pours out of me just by looking at each of you. So today I wanted to acknowledge that on any one day I can have moments when I feel like I'm totally boshing this parenting malarkey, and others when I feel like I'm failing at it.

And I think that's OK.

Yours always,
Mumma xx

HEARD FROM THE FRONT SEAT —
BIG, MEDIUM, SMALL

Dear Buzz,

Today you had this conversation with Buddy.

Buzz: Buddy, I'm big, because I was born first.

Buddy: No, I'm big.

Buzz: No, I'm big, you're medium and Max is small because he was born last. You're medium because you're in the middle.
(*Big pause – I can't see Buddy's face in the mirror but can see you looking at him, reading his expression.*)

Buzz: You're medium, and that's the best one! It's the best one! Because you're big *and* small. You're both. I wish I was medium.

You don't wish you were medium, not at all, but you watched your little brother's face drop as you spoke and tried your best to flip it around so that he would see the bonuses of being the middle child, neither the biggest nor the smallest.

You totally sold it to him.

I had to stop the lump in my throat turning into an almighty sob. This is something I know Buddy has been finding increasingly difficult to deal with, which I never really thought he would. I guess that's where the whole middle-child thing comes from – you're not the biggest but the role of baby-in-the-family has been taken away from you. You're in child limbo, trying to work out where that leaves you. I've been doing a lot of thinking about Buddy's behaviour lately and how I can help him feel more secure, loved and happy. He is not a bad child (if there is such a thing). He is full of gentleness and has an amazing admiration for nature – he's a natural nurturer, so it's been heartbreaking to see him lashing out physically, verbally and emotionally. But I'm starting to understand the confusion and hurt that's going on in his brain, and know that your dad and I have to be more patient with him and give him more of our time. We have to get to know his triggers and how to help him process his feelings while reassuring him.

In this snippet of a chat you were doing just that. You were maturely recognizing that your words were upsetting him and making a shift in your delivery.

I know the two of you squabble a lot, but when you play together and have conversations like this, where you're both really listening and responding, I feel so incredibly proud.

Thanks for today, Buzz. Thanks for reminding me that we can all do our bit to ensure we feel supported and loved within this family unit.

Love you,
Mumma xx

NIGHT-TIME HORROR!

....

Dear Buddy,

I'm racking my brains to work out when this started, but during the night you regularly wake up calling to us and screaming. In we run, ready to be by your side and comfort you, wondering if you've had a bad dream or fallen out of bed, but it's no use. You are somewhere else. Our reassuring hands are like fire on your skin – your mind sure that we're hurting you with even the gentlest of touches.

You are agitated, scared, hysterical and violent. Tears stream down your face as you say words that make no sense.

A night terror. You are not quite asleep, yet not quite awake. You're somewhere else and there's nothing we can do to help you but keep you safe from lashing out and hurting yourself. Standing back and watching you in that state is the hardest thing.

Some nights I hold you close despite your protests, repeating over and over in your ear, 'Mumma's here. You're safe, Buddy. I love you, Buddy.' Just a whisper, but I hope it gets through. You're rigid and fraught, but I need to get you back here, and away from whatever it is you think you're experiencing. Away from what's upsetting you so terribly.

The craziest part of all is that both Buzz and Max sleep through all the noise unless it's past 5 a.m. and

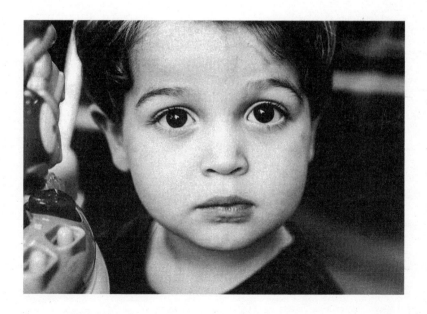

close to when they usually wake up anyway. It's as though their ears are switched off to your noise. This is bonkers, considering you and Buzz share a room and sleep just a couple of feet away from each other. You are literally screaming in his ear and he doesn't even flinch!

Adrenalin pumps through my body while I long for you to come back to me – my body soft but firm, comforting but strong. Eventually the shouts subside. You suddenly stop, easing into my touch, your body dropping into mine. Your screams becoming whimpers until you fall into silence – as though you're shell-shocked and confused, unsure what's been going on and visibly shaken.

I honestly believe you have no control or awareness during these episodes, so to see that level of anger and anguish flying from you makes me so sad. I often wonder what effect it has on you to have these experiences, even if you aren't fully aware of them afterwards.

You cling to me while I cover you with kisses, happy you escaped.

I hold you until your breathing has slowed, and you've fallen back to sleep. Relieved it's over.

Mumma xx

To my wonderful Mum and Dad,

Almost two decades ago you made a decision that would alter life for all of us. Between Christmas and New Year 2001, you separated. I can't remember all of it. It's a patch of time that my mind has suppressed. I think I was sitting on the bed when someone told me what was happening, but I can't be sure of that.

Were you aware that we'd sit at the top of the stairs when you argued? That we'd look at each other and wonder whether our family unit was going to break? That we feared being asked to choose between you both? That we'd cry at the thought of our lives changing, before swiftly running into our separate bedrooms as soon as we heard you heading out into the hallway?

When I could hear you screaming at each other I wanted to tell you to stop. When I could hear you howling in despair from the lounge, I wanted so much to go down and offer hugs. When one of you left for a walk to cool down, I'd sit at my window and wonder if you'd return.

After you separated and I'd left home to go to drama school, I'd have nights where I would call you both, hear how lonely you were, and question whether being alone and miserable apart was really any better than being unhappy together.

I didn't get it, but then the love stories in the books I read and the films I watched always resulted in a happy ending. My new reality didn't look like that.

I felt sad, I felt lost, and I know I felt resentment for the tampering with our perfect family picture. It was a selfish view, but teenagers are generally selfish, temperamental and unreasonable towards their

parents anyway. I guess you just gave me more ammo to be a bit of a twerp.

I don't think I fully realized how much of a wrench it must have been for you both to end a marriage after twenty years. To change the course of our family, to sell our home, to lose some of your friends, to feel that people were talking about you, to part from the person you turned to for everything (even though you argued), to tip your whole life the wrong way up and find a new way of being – and then the guilt that must have been there because of us kids. The decision to stay together or be apart was more loaded than ever because of us. We made things more complicated because, despite being apart, you would never get a clean break or be free of one another. We would be, and have continued to be, the superglue that forces you to remain in each other's lives.

It was a horrible time back then, uncomfortable as we got used to our new normal and tried to work out how to function as a dysfunctional family. It was never going to be easy. The first time we forced you to be together (a birthday, I think) was always going to be tense, and there were always going to be words said that caused an atmosphere or made us all aware of the grief we were suffering.

But as the years rolled by we eventually met your new partners (there have been some interesting choices in that time, but I think you've both finally cracked it), learnt to adapt and be together in this new way, inviting new faces into the fold.

Somehow you stuck at it, never giving up on us as a collective.

I know families who've been through what we have and never recovered. They haven't found a way to forgive the heartache and move on, or at least accept that the other will always be a part of their lives.

People are shocked when they find out you are

divorced but still able to be together and talk – even
spend Christmas Day together.

You're friends, but I'm not naïve enough not to
think that the biggest reason you've ploughed through

the hurt and remained in each other's lives is us, your children.

Therefore, this letter is to thank you. Thank you for not bringing us into your disputes and using us as pawns. Thank you for pushing forwards and finding a way to be civil, then letting a friendship grow. Thank you for not giving up on us. Thank you for putting your love for us first.

Our set-up isn't what any of us thought or hoped it would be, but how lucky we are to have a family like ours.

We work.

And that is because of you!

Thank you for showing me that there is not one way to be a family, and that even when things don't go as you'd planned, you can still find laughter, love and happiness.

Love you!
Giovanna xx

WHAT MAKES YOU HAPPY?

Me: Buzz, what makes you happy?'

Buzz: Playing with Lego.

Me: What else?

Buzz: Building Lego.

Me: What else?

Buzz: Playing and building Lego with Dadda.

Me: Anything that's not related to Lego? What would make you happy?

Buzz: Playing with Dadda and him going really small like Ant-Man . . . Then I could play with him in my Lego.

175

Me: I see . . . Do you want to know what makes me happy?

Buzz: No.

Thanks, Bubs!
Mumma xx

MAMA, MUMMA, MUMMY, MUM . . .
A progression of names. All me. All from you.

....

Dear Boys,

It might sound strange but I feel like I found my
identity when you were born. I have no problem when
people call me 'Buzz's mum' instead of Gi or
Giovanna. I love being called that. In many ways that
is the simplest and most meaningful role I have, and
sometimes I wish that was my only identity and my
sole focus.

I guess the big shift I feel constrained by in my new
role is the responsibility and lack of spontaneity.
Going for a walk takes organization, seeing friends
takes planning and consideration – even my morning
poo has to be negotiated around where you all are and
which child should come with me.

I also don't remember the last day I had where I
didn't encounter a little bit of stress and drama while

someone had a meltdown about something seemingly trivial to the outsider but humongously important to one of you – like wearing the 'right' pair of white socks, even though they're all identical, or the fact your banana has broken in half. I don't have days where I just laze about and sit in silence. I have to be switched on and ready to act. I have to be in mum mode, caring, thinking, planning and doing at all times.

No wonder people suffer with feeling they've lost their sense of self. No wonder there's such a big emphasis on the importance of me-time and doing the things you enjoy outside the house. I always thought a loss of identity in motherhood meant somehow resenting being known through your child, rather than for your own quirks and sparkles, but now I understand. Now I relate.

I don't remember the last time I did something without serious planning and checking in with someone else first – including going for a shower in the morning. 'Are you OK if I go for a shower now?' I ask your dad, checking on what you three are up to and whether it's safe to leave – knowing he'll be doing exactly the same in thirty minutes' time.

That's another thing. I now take no longer than half an hour to get ready – sometimes I manage it in less (around twenty minutes) if I'm not drying my hair or putting on make-up, and the majority of the time I'm aware of how long I'm taking and feel a certain heaviness thinking about what you might be doing below me, and whether you're being challenging for your dad. I know he can deal with any situation that arises, probably better than I can, but something in me carries guilt and a sense of responsibility.

Anyway, I've reached that point in motherhood where I'm crying out for me-time.

I've taken up running regularly since the London Vitality run with Bryony Gordon and the girls, and I now do five kilometres each time I go out – which I try to do every other day. I wouldn't say I actually enjoy the running part. I spend most of the time wondering when I'm going to start loving what I'm putting my body through as it always feels like such a struggle, but there's something about being out of the house on my own, listening to podcasts of other adults talking, that gives me some peace, or maybe it's the opposite. Perhaps it's actually reactivating my brain, taking me out of the parental overwhelm and back to the basics of putting one foot in front of the other. In those moments I'm not thinking about anything but the task in hand. My responsibilities are on hold.

Today I smashed my target and achieved my first ever sub-30 run, which means I ran five kilometres in less than thirty minutes. It was a close call as I did it in twenty-nine minutes and twenty-seven seconds, but I still did it. It made me so emotional. I wasn't running four months ago, so to beat a target I set myself was incredible. I cried.

The weeks I don't run, when I'm on a deadline, your dad is away, or I simply can't carve out that half an hour to myself, I can start to feel blue, snappy and overwhelmed. It's an unsettling feeling yet I know it's my body and mind screaming out for those endorphins to be released.

Generally it's my workload and not family life that stresses me out. My brain can feel cloudy and bogged down, but a run clears that and lightens the load, even though nothing has changed in the half-hour I've been away. Plus, knowing I can run anywhere when I leave the house has put a little spontaneity back into my life.

I think running might make me a better wife and mother! When I come back I feel depleted yet replenished, and ready to lose myself in the role of mummy!

Love you!
Mumma xx

Dear Boys,

Today I was wearing a top from Mutha.Hood. It has three words on the front, and in a moment of calm (it doesn't happen very often but it's amazing when it does), while all three of you were sitting still and having a snack, Buzz asked what they said. I held the fabric away from my chest so that the words lay flat,

allowing you to read them: 'Strong Girls Club'.

'Are you in a club?' asked Buzz – in hindsight I realize you were probably comparing it to the clubs at school, which was why you found it funny that I was in one.

'Yes,' I said proudly. 'I'm in a club with strong girls.'

Buzz looked at me, his eyes widening a little, the corners of his mouth twitching. Buddy observed the exchange with his usual disapproving frown while deep in thought, and Max was lost in the task of inhaling his bright orange corn snack.

'Do you show them how to be strong?' Buzz asked, really trying to understand.

'Girls are already strong,' I replied, loving the fact that you'd given me the role of teacher – suggesting you already considered me a strong girl. Or perhaps because I'm a woman you automatically considered I'd be the one telling little girls what to do – just like your teachers do in cookery and ballet.

'Boys are stronger,' he replied, his expression one of deep thought as he inspected the food in his hand. 'When I'm a grown-up, I'm going to be big and strong so I can protect the person I marry.'

The words made me smile. Marriage has become a big topic in your class at the moment, and you've put quite a lot of thought into who and where. You were pretty set on one person, then two, before eventually listing most of the people in your class that you would marry if you could – girls, boys, everyone was included. Yet in this particular moment

you'd reverted to just the one spouse and just the one wedding.

'You know, Mummy protects Daddy sometimes too,' I offered, wanting to give this chat a bit of balance and show you that strength comes in lots of guises.

'That's because you're strong,' you stated.

Needless to say, I smiled in reply before becoming distracted as hands started grabbing at other people's snacks and I got dragged into refereeing a negotiation.

Sitting at my desk I'm mulling over the comments.

I'm not worried about you boys getting on with girls and understanding that we're all equal. Not in the slightest. You most definitely play with the girls in your classes just as much as you do with the boys. You have a deep affection for them and talk about them often. You haven't automatically beelined for the familiar – which is something I think could easily happen in a house of three boys. Yet as more and more focus is being put on labels and how we talk to and about each other, I feel I have to be more aware so that you don't fall into the same traps that have been laid out for us all over the majority of our history.

In terms of physical strength, yes. I think it's fair to generalize and say most men are physically stronger than most women. However, there are many other ways a person can be strong, regardless of sex. Strength comes in skills, talents, knowledge and humility. In making yourself heard while being ready to listen. In being willing to compromise and apologize. In knowing who you are and understanding your beliefs, while not being threatened by or disrespectful of those held by others, which might conflict with your own. In being able to show emotion

without feeling self-conscious or 'weak'. In being proud to be you, and rejoicing in everything you are, rather than wasting time comparing yourself to another person's successes.

So, yes, it's great that some people can do chin-ups or dead-lift 500 kilos – and let's not take away the talent, time and dedication those two physical challenges require to achieve – but let's stop putting limits on strength and change the dialogue a little.

You are not weak if you fail.

You are not weak if you compromise.

You are not weak if you cry.

Be you, and always be led by love. I know that might sound a tad wanky, and I truly apologize for being an embarrassing mum, but I want you all to be led by kindness and compassion, not to think only about yourselves. Think, rather, about how your actions can affect others.

I feel like I've welcomed three boys at an odd part of our history. We're told that now is the time for women. We're being shown examples of abuse, of women being taken advantage of purely because of their sex, of women being suppressed, ignored, belittled and pushed aside. Finally women are taking back their voices. Shouting louder. Standing taller. Reaching higher. Finally women are no longer afraid to take their places at work, sharing their 'places' in the home. Finally things are being questioned. Why me? Why not him? Why him? Why not me? As a woman I have felt empowered by this change, or at least fired up by what it could mean for my future. Then I had you three boys and suddenly slogans like 'The future is female' left me scratching my head a little. I have felt myself wonder, *What about you?*

As a parent you want your child to be a part of

society, accepted and loved by the world around them, so I think this is a natural feeling to experience when your child is in the 51 per cent of the population deemed to be the problem. I want you to know the future is *yours* too. I want you to know you are also strong, independent, and can change the world . . . and I want you to know that the problem isn't you, and that as a child you can work hard and dream big to be whoever you want to be, just like everybody else.

Right now the issue is beyond you. It has nothing to do with the men you will grow up to become. It's decades and centuries of women having no rights and lower pay, and of being deemed the 'weaker' sex. Moving forward, there are patterns that need to be broken. For change to come about, a noise has to be made, fingers have to be pointed and people must be blamed. There needs to be a reassessing of order, balance and power to obtain equality.

I've come to realize it's not a case of one sex ruling, it's about being in it *together*. Of making change *together*. So, boys, let's use all of our various strengths and be part of that change. Let's look at others and, regardless of their race, gender, sexuality, beliefs and upbringing, think, What can I do for you? and act on those impulses. Let's be the best versions of ourselves and be ready to question anything that seems degrading or disrespectful to others.

Tonight, while Buddy was having a little meltdown, I asked him what was in his heart, trying to remind him of a chat we had earlier about kindness and compassion. Before he could answer, with the anticipated 'love', Buzz jumped in to help. 'Blood,' he stated. Well, there's no arguing with that, Buzz. But let the blood pump the love through every single bit of you.

I love you!
Yours, Mumma xxx

Dear Mum and Dad,

One thing you always did, which I will treasure for ever, was kiss me goodnight when you came upstairs to bed. Dad, you also kissed us goodbye before you left for work in the early hours of the morning. It's something I love thinking of you doing, and I now do with my own boys. I couldn't imagine getting into bed and not checking on them, kissing them (probably a bit firmer than I should, seeing as I want them to stay asleep) and whispering that I love them. I do

that because you did it to me, and on the odd occasion that I woke up I'd always feel such a warm loved feeling. I want to pass that on – even if it means risking waking them up and angering them, resulting in them grunting at me while shrugging me off. I'll take that.

Your night-time kisses didn't always quite go to plan, though, did they, Dad? One night when you came upstairs I was still awake, busy wobbling my front tooth, which was sure to fall out soon. We were giggling about something and then you pretended to knock my wobbly peg out . . . except you managed to make contact with it, resulting in it breaking free and landing between us on the bed. You were mortified. Yet, for some reason the Tooth Fairy was good to me that night – very generous – so I couldn't complain.

You were both very affectionate. Dad, you would even reach back behind yourself and grab our ankles while driving, as though you had been missing us from the front seat and just wanted to connect with us. It's something I do now when we're sitting at traffic lights.

Mum, your approach was more like you were getting us into a head lock, a little more rigid as you clamped

hold of us and gave us a squeeze, playfully holding us
tightly so that we couldn't move and protest.

We are a very tactile family and always have
been. We hug, we kiss (on the cheek) and we
occasionally wrestle (this is mostly Mario and me).
I didn't realize this affection wasn't the norm until
we met other families who didn't even hug in
greeting or whenever they were passing one another –
who could literally say goodbye and walk out of the
front door without a farewell cuddle. The sight was
alien to me.

All I can say is that a hug from any of you (yes,
Mum, even with you and your slightly too aggressive
embrace) can make a grey day better. A hug can heal,
someone stepping in to comfort and support when
words fail.

My boys love hugging and I hope they never stop.
I love it too. I wonder what other things have been
passed on and what traditions we've started, what
they'll look back on fondly and think, She loved us;
She put the towels on the radiator for when we got out
the bath, she loved us; She always spent time on the
beach digging in the sand, she loved us; She stayed
with us while we fell asleep even though she had loads
of work to do downstairs, she loved us . . .

I remember watching a segment on *Good Morning Britain* a few years ago about boys and their families, and about how when they get to a certain age the public displays of affection stop. This made me feel sick with worry. When will the kisses and cuddles come to an end? Will it be sudden? Will they push me away and shrug me off? Will my heart actually break at the rebuff? Or will it just happen less and less until it ceases to occur at all, without any of us really noticing it? Will I be hit with the realization one day that they aren't my little babies any more?

I worry about these things. I worry about there being a loss of connection, and the push and pull of teenage years. But then I see Giorgina, Mario and me with you and feel a sense of hope, possibly even excitement. I'm five foot four now, and I'll probably shrink a bit with age, so it's highly likely all three of my boys will be taller than me. The thought of the first time they'll lay their arm across my shoulders, instead of mine across theirs, puts me in a place of awe for what's to come.

Mum and Dad, you've shown me the importance of affection and the comfort in declaring your love in a physical way. I know our family set-up isn't one any of us would've chosen, seeing as you're no longer together, but it's fair to say we've made the most of it.

Right, better go – the kids are in bed and I want to hold Buddy's hand for a moment or two while he's asleep and can't wriggle away from me.

I love you both!
Giovanna (one of your favourite daughters) xx

I'M NOT PERFECT AND NEITHER ARE YOU . . . AND THAT'S JUST PERFECT!

Dear Boys,

OK, this is going to surprise you, but I have flaws. Big ones. I mean, nothing so big that you're going to be rocked to your core but big enough for you to know I'm a real human, with strengths and weaknesses, successes and failures. I'm not perfect and I don't always get it right – as you've witnessed on occasions when I've lost my shit, sworn in front of you (like the time I broke my middle toe – who breaks their MIDDLE toe?!) or burnt the dinner.

I'm telling you this because I want you to celebrate the things that make you the people you are. I want you to embrace that person and see what they have to offer, rather than worry about what they might lack.

There are going to be times when I disappoint you. And the first time it really sinks in that I don't get things right all the time, or that I'm just making it up as I go along without having all the answers, is going to suck for you. It'll be like realizing a fictional character you've loved all your life isn't real – but that's reality.

One day you will see through me, and I hope that doesn't set free resentment, or sadness. Nature seems to encourage you to see your dad and me as flawless individuals, perched high on pedestals for you to try to impress. People to listen to, admire and respect – and that happens without us even forcing the issue.

I want you to know that perfection doesn't exist.

We will all make mistakes and disappoint ourselves or others. It is inevitable. Yes, you have to try hard in life and make the most of opportunities that come your way – but I never want you to feel so bogged down with pressure that things become too much. I never want you to think your failures would make us love you any less. You are also flawed, and that's OK.

I accept and love every single bit of you – even if
I won't always like it. I can say that because you won't
always like the things I do either.

   I've seen parents who have lost their sons talking
on *This Morning.* People who clearly loved and
supported their sons so very much. As a mum of
boys, I can't help but wonder what is happening that
makes young men feel their lives aren't worth living.
I wonder why all the love and support their parents
gave them wasn't enough. Those sons were snatched

away prematurely, and a lifetime of what-ifs plagues their parents' grief.

If we argue, know that nothing will ever be irreparable.

If we fight, know that you can always say sorry and that I will accept your apology.

If you do something you deem bad, know I'm always there to listen without judgement.

If you feel you've failed, know that that particular incident does not eclipse the life you have already lived or the other successes waiting ahead of you.

If you feel like you have nothing, know that I am always your something. Know that you are always my everything.

If you feel like the only option you have is to skip to the last page of your book, know that we are here waiting to start more chapters and explore more worlds with you.

When you watched films as kids, you were always frightened of the scary or sad bits. Sometimes you'd say you didn't want to watch it any more, but we'd always encourage you to carry on, wanting you to understand that you have to make it through the bad moments to see the good again. I know it's easy to say with movies, which all have a narrative arc, but I hope

I'm Not Perfect and Neither Are You . . . and That's Just Perfect!

you manage to see through the tough times your lives will be peppered with.

Ask for help.

Talk.

My whole heart aches at the thought of the alternative.

I love you so much!
Mumma xx

Dearest Buddy,

You have taken to enjoying company when you're on the loo. Occasionally you'll want the opposite and you'll shout for us to leave you be, but at the moment you love an audience – especially if it's Summer Rae, your cheeky accomplice of a cousin, who will gladly follow you anywhere.

Today I was the lucky spectator as you pushed out a number two, and this was our conversation. You did not skip a beat with your answers.

Buddy: When are we going to the park?

Me: After Mummy and Daddy have had showers.

Buddy: I want a shower.

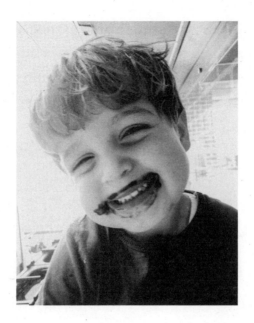

Me: You could have a shower with Mummy?

Buddy: I want to shower with Dadda.
  (*Of course you do — you always want what's not offered.*)

Me: Why don't you have a shower with Mumma?

Buddy: I don't like your boobies. Or your foofoo . . .
  Or your nose.

I would like to say you stopped there, but you actually

went on to list more of my parts. I gasped at each insult, causing you to giggle into your hands.

You got your shower with Dadda, and my heart was warmer from our little interaction. You might think you won – but I got to have a quick tidy up before we went out *and* I got to shower in peace. *Thank you!*

Love,
My foofoo, and my boobies, and my nose, and my mouth, and my legs, and my ears, and my arms, and all the other parts that come together to form your mumma xx

LOVE GROWTH

Boys,

Having three children is
tough on the heart and mind.
I believe that with each child
the chambers of my heart
have grown, allowing the
amount of love it can hold to
increase with each new arrival.
It was something I fretted
about. How could I be so
devoted to the newbie when my
heart already belonged so
unconditionally to another? But
my body and mind had that all
figured out. There was no need to
feel torn. Love can multiply in

ways I never knew before motherhood, or before I
held each of you in my arms and found out what I was
capable of. I have had to learn to adapt that love to
each of your needs – because each of you requires my
love, reassurance and encouragement in different
ways.

Another concern was how you would react to a new
baby in the house, and if you would feel put out by our
attention being divided and shared. If I'm honest, that
is something we're still aware of, and we'll always be
making sure you all feel reassured, wanted and
secure . . . It feels like a balancing act, and whenever
one of you acts up I feel a pang in my heart at the
thought that it is probably just a cry for attention.

Oh, the mum-guilt!

Well, tonight we've been watching videos from
when we brought Max home from the hospital and
you all huddled together for the first time. Say what
you want about technology and the obsession for
recording every single detail of life, but I would've
forgotten amazing details had they not been filmed.
Buzz, you were wearing the biggest grin as we walked
through the door with Max in his car seat. You were
literally bouncing on the spot while you waited for us
to take him out so you could see him better. Then you

dived on to the sofa and started preparing the cushions so that you could hold him in your arms.

Buddy, you were asleep when we arrived. You came down from your nap a little while later in a quiet and uncertain mood, observing the peaceful scene, and the bundle in your nana's arms. Your reluctance was hardly surprising: you had a massive wound on your head and had been on your own adventure with Nana and Ewad. We kept things calm, allowing you to watch and engage in your own time.

When you eventually held Max you were so gentle. You knew how precious he was and you adapted your

touch accordingly as you planted the gentlest of kisses on his head and stroked his hand.

There are more videos following that first encounter. More kisses, more cuddles, more images captured of Max in your arms after you'd asked to hold him.

My heart melted all over again, looking through the videos and pictures. Funny that when I look back at something you did in the past it can make me love you more in the present.

With Max on the move now you frequently forget

that he is not as able as you – that he is still more fragile and unsteady, that he still needs taking care of, for you to use your gentle hands and give him soft kisses.

There are times when I feel in complete despair because you've been too rough with your baby brother, or have purposely gone out of your way to do something you know will hurt him – like picking him up and clumsily putting him down, or peeling his fingers away from a chair he's holding on to. But . . . you're all learning, and I see the utter joy on your faces when you do something to make him laugh or when he leans towards you for a kiss.

Buzz and Buddy, I thought you'd be over the excitement of having a baby brother by now, but you really aren't. The novelty hasn't worn off, and the pride and amazement on your faces when he does something new, like crawl or stand up on his own, are adorable.

I have no doubt that you'll continue to fight and squabble growing up – especially when Max learns to stick up for himself – but I hope that the love you have continues to grow and deepen. The three of you will understand each other in a way we won't be able to, and I hope you'll not only go on lots of adventures together but be there for and confide in one another when you need it.

Three brothers.
Three *amigos.*
Your own little tripod, giving each other strength and support.
Aren't we so blooming lucky?

Mumma xx

Dear Boys,

Every evening I go into your bedrooms to give you a kiss goodnight. One particular evening I'd popped my head in because someone had called. It was darker than normal, though, and you'd gone quiet so I thought I'd brush my teeth before kissing you – giving you longer to settle back to sleep so that I didn't wake you up properly.

When I came back in I nearly had a heart attack.

Buddy was not in his bed. He was not on his floor. As far as I could tell he was not in the room. I ran out of the door and had a quick look downstairs in case he'd trotted off while I was in the bathroom. Nope. Nowhere.

Back to your bedroom I went, my heart starting to race.

Looking around the room again, I glanced at Buzz in his bed and had a further fright: something wasn't quite right.

That was when I noticed two heads of hair on the one pillow. Looking closer and allowing my eyes to adjust, I saw you lying next to each other. My guess is that Buddy had fallen out of bed or was scared (which explains what I heard), then decided to get into bed with Buzz for comfort.

Oh, my heart!

I watched you for a bit, then called your dad in to

take a look. We even hugged to celebrate the miracle –
the wonder of creation before us.

Too cute.

I went to bed, a lightness in my chest at knowing
you were being so loving. As with all moments of
calm and tenderness in motherhood, you have to
make the most of it while it lasts . . . Ten minutes later
I woke up to you arguing. Buzz, you'd obviously
woken to find Buddy in your bed and weren't too
pleased.

Jumping between each other's beds hasn't
happened since – but there was one night when you'd
both decided to come into our room. I think we'd just
got back from Florida so your body clocks were all
over the shop. You were both in the bed when I went
to feed Max in the early hours of the morning. When
I came back you were properly snuggled into each
other – your limbs entwined and your faces pressed
together. I had to marvel at the sight before climbing
in next to you . . . not that you'd left me much space.

When you want to be, you guys are so darn cute!

Love you,
Mumma xx

To the mum in the waiting room,

Today I had to take Buzz to see the doctor because he has been having coughing fits when running around and regularly wakes up in the night with one. Asthma, clearly. And although these symptoms have been there for a long time (possibly years), I've only just realized the pattern and thought to get it checked. Tom took Buzz to the walk-in centre a couple of days ago after a hairy night with coughing fits to confirm our suspicions, and today I had to take Buzz for a follow-up with our GP.

It felt quite the luxury strolling into the waiting room with just the one child – the oldest one too. He's reasonable (most of the time) and was thrilled to find a Marvel superhero activity book in the kids' box. He grabbed it straight away and started flicking through it to see what he could read. He even attempted his first word search, although he wouldn't listen to any of my advice on how to scour the tables efficiently (place your finger in the top left corner, then work your way along each row).

I became acutely aware of how calm I felt while out with one of my children. I felt like a mother in control . . . It was relaxing and peaceful. My limbs weren't full of adrenalin, ready to race after a child on the run or pounce on a baby about to fall into a table corner. It was a lovely sensation to revel in momentarily.

While Buzz was preoccupied with his book and I was busy feeling like a composed mother, I looked up and noticed you and your family. You and your partner (I'm assuming) were there with your baby and toddler. I'm guessing your daughter was around one, and your son closer to three. You'd clearly been

waiting a while although, let's be frank, sometimes two minutes can feel like thirty if you have a restless child with you. Your son was visibly fed up with waiting and toddled around the room with you or your partner close by while the other held the baby.

It was only us in the waiting room, and I must

admit that I do have a tendency to people-watch when I'm out and about. I'm a writer. Observations are important to my craft. That said, I don't remember watching you too much, and Buzz kept pulling my attention to his book anyway. He'd found the word *Krull* (some baddie from some other planet, I dunno).

The moment I looked up, though, I caught sight of your son running towards your daughter who'd just been placed on the floor. All three of us adults clocked it, but couldn't intervene before he made contact with her chest, causing her to fall backwards and hit her head with an almighty thud.

'No!' one of you said, as you rushed in to get her, picking her up and rubbing her head. Taking her away from danger.

Your face told me it wasn't the first time that had happened. Your face told me you were anxious about what it meant. Your face told me you were embarrassed by the behaviour.

'I have three,' I heard myself say. 'Five, three and eleven months. And the three-year-old keeps doing that.'

I wanted you to hear it. Because seeing your son act in the same way towards his sibling as one of mine does gave me a sense of relief and I wanted you to feel

that too. You are not the only one who feels you can't put your child down for fear of what your other child might do. You are not the only one whose child is like a bull in a china shop. You are not the only one feeling sad about their roughness. You are not the only one willing your child to be nice. You are not the only one feeling scared, confused and frustrated, wondering if it's something you've done. It's so disheartening when all you want them to do is love each other.

And so I realize it's not just me. And it's not just me and *you*. There will be so many children acting in this way, and so many mothers feeling lost about what to do. We have not gone wrong. I'm sure, for all our sakes, that this is just a stage. That soon enough they'll stop behaving in that way – possibly only when our babies are old enough to hit back, causing us to notch up our refereeing skills a gear.

I write books about motherhood, and often get asked whether *Happy Mum, Happy Baby* will be followed up with *Happy Toddler, Happy Mum* (let's be clear – *Happy Toddler* would definitely go first: toddlers rule the roost!) – but there's no way I could write a book about the frustrations of children of that age without feeling I was betraying trust at a time when they're learning, discovering and tackling huge developmental stages. Even now that Buddy has transitioned from a toddler to an early pre-schooler, it would feel wrong. I don't want him to be labelled as difficult or bad. He's just a child who is learning, as all children do. And I tell myself that I never had this with Buzz, but that's not true. Those memories have just been replaced. They're learning.

I guess the point of this letter isn't to say, 'They all do it, so let them get on with bashing their younger siblings around', but more 'You're not on your own'. It's about seeing you reassured that this is just a phase. So we can continue to guide them and encourage them to show love, while being comforted by the fact it's not them or us. It's life. It's feelings and emotions. It's love, fear and understanding. Holding on to that thought might help us handle better the situations we find ourselves in.

I hope this makes sense . . . If it's any help, when I got home with Buzz one of my best friends came over and experienced the height of witching-hour hell. I didn't even have the energy or time to be embarrassed. There I was, using my full-on calm voice, while trying to remember exactly what I was meant to be saying if I wasn't shouting at them to stop or sending them to the thinking step.

We'll get there. Right?

Big love,
Giovanna (the mum who looked like she was totally nailing this motherhood thing, but was only in possession of 33.3 per cent of her charges when you saw her) xx

Dear Boys,

When the time came for Buzz and Buddy to start
sharing a room, I decided to get
you new beds. Buzz, you had a cool
tent-type bed, but it was impractical
to think we'd have two of them in
one room. To make the most of the
space and for it to function best, you
needed something simpler.

Scrolling through different designs
was easy enough, yet the more I
looked the more I felt the magnitude
of what I was doing, and the more
overwhelmed I became. I called your
dad over to show him the options, then
wept uncontrollably.

I literally sobbed at the thought of having two beds side by side and you sleeping in them, despite it being my idea. Having two of my children sleeping in proper beds felt so very grown-up. It's funny how the smallest things can have such a huge impact on your heart, perhaps because we spend so long preparing ourselves for the big ones that the smaller catch us off-guard. We all know the first day of school is tough. We all know the first time they spend the night with grandparents is weird. I'm sure I'll be a wreck the first time you go away on a school trip. But little changes within the home that symbolize the end of one chapter and the start of another cause tears to spring to my eyes too. As do the little acts of independence and maturity you suddenly surprise me with. Like when you help me tidy up without moaning (and prove yourself to be very helpful), when you read me a book and know words like 'atmosphere' (it was a book on space), and when you create a whole world while playing peacefully together, allowing me to sit and have a hot cup of coffee (still rare, but amazing when it happens). All these things highlight how far you've come from the squawky little baby boys I brought home from hospital.

I cry because certain moments are over. Transitions

are happening, often without us even realizing. One day we just stop doing things. There's no big song and dance, but midnight loo trips end, night feeds disappear, stair gates are taken off . . . One day you'll kiss me on the lips for the last time, and before that, I'll pick you up for the last time too – and I won't even know to take in the moment and commit it to memory.

I'll cry again when the time comes to put Max in a proper bed, knowing that move will also mean getting rid of the cot and the last of the baby bits as we properly exit the baby zone. Even though I know it'll pull on my heartstrings and make my ovaries ache, I'm looking forward to moving beyond this stage, away from breast-pumps and changing mats.

You all seem to think you're getting a triple bunk-bed when it's Max's turn to venture out of his cot, and I can just imagine Buddy clambering up and down the ladder morning and night. However, I would prefer to lessen our chances of ending up back in A and E with more head injuries.

Oh, gosh, I'll be getting you double beds before I know it.

My heart can't cope with that thought just yet.

All my love,
Mumma xx

ONE DRINK AND I SHRINK!

Dear Boys,

You think I have a drinking problem. Your dad and I were being silly one night and taking photos where it looked like I was inside his glass of wine. This mesmerized you, Buzz and Buddy. Your eyes widened in disbelief.

'How'd you get so small?' Buzz asked, while Buddy just gawped from the photo to me.

'I shrink when I have red wine, Bubba.' I shrugged, as if it was a normal occurrence and not something I'd made up for entertainment.

Buzz and Buddy, you both looked back at the photo
with wonderment and awe, totally amazed as you took
in my words as fact, as though you'd just discovered
something fascinating about me.

Seconds later you wandered off, distracted.
I thought you'd seen through my tall tale and known it
was nonsense. However, a few nights later you were
poorly, Buzz. Wandering down the stairs looking pale,
clammy and dishevelled, you joined us on the sofa for

a cuddle and we got you some medicine. While
waiting, you observed the remnants of the treats we'd
been devouring – a bar of dark orange Lindt chocolate
and two wine glasses.

'Mumma,' you whispered with urgency, 'you're not
small.'

'Huh?' I said, ready to dose him up with Calpol and
wondering if being poorly and sleepy was making him
a little delusional.

'You're drinking red wine! You haven't shrunk!'

I twigged then. Oh, how I howled!

Love, your average-sized
Mumma xx

SLEEP IS EVERYTHING!

Dear Sons,

Everyone tells me that by the time you're in your teens I'm going to be pulling my hair out trying to get you out of bed. I find that idea ironic and bewildering, seeing as your dad and I have spent so much of our parenting life to date worrying about nap-times, bedtimes and early rising. I don't think we have ever all remained in bed past 7 a.m.

I love my sleep. I could and can sleep anywhere. Seriously, I'm pretty sure I've slept standing up before – probably with one of you in my arms in the middle of the night during the newborn stages.

There were also times in those early days when I'd
wake up in a panic patting at my chest, sure I'd fallen
asleep while feeding you. The fear that you'd vanished
or that I'd crushed you would fill me with dread. Of
course, a look to my right always told me the truth and
filled me with relief. There you would be, fast asleep,
exactly where I'd placed you in your cot beside me a
short while before.

That's exhaustion for you. It stops you being able to
function properly as you try technique after technique
to get your baby to sleep. It was during those sleepless
nights, when it was dark and cold outside, that I was at
my loneliest and most vulnerable, especially in the
early days of parenthood. I just felt weak,
overwhelmed, and was continuously berating myself
for being rubbish at motherhood.

Buzz, your dad spotted me on many occasions
standing in the middle of the room with my eyes shut,
trying to sway you to sleep while tears streamed down
my face – that I couldn't sway to any sort of rhythm
highlighted how tired I was.

I used to count, telling myself you'd be asleep by
the time I got to sixty. When you weren't I'd just loop
around again. And again. And again. Zero to sixty at
the slowest pace ever, all the while bouncing or

swaying. Time and time again I'd feel like I'd cracked it, only to open my eyes and see you frowning at me.

All three of you grew out of that baby stage of broken sleep within a few months and became far more comfortable in being able to settle yourselves without needing us to rock or bounce you – although a trip to Australia with Buzz when he was ten months old completely ruined that for two years!

The night feeds were tough, and something that Max kept up for the longest (it was the last of his feeds to go after his first birthday), but by the end I'd only be up for ten minutes or so at around three in the morning, which didn't seem too strenuous. After a year of being the one having to get up, though (I'm the one with the baps), I was ready for your dad to take over, getting out of bed and going in to reassure and settle Max.

Even now, unless he has a difficult or important workday ahead – like playing the O2 – I give him a big elbow or shake to make sure he's awake and has heard the call for us. Part of me feels bad and guilty, until I remember the number of nights it was me leaving the bed and I snuggle into my duvet.

Before having Buzz I can remember a mate of ours saying how incredible those night feeds are when it's

just you and your baby awake and you can soak them up in the stillness. In the newborn stages I didn't see the beauty in it at all. Not first-time round. I was stressed and my boobs hurt so much. As time has gone by I have grown fond of them, aware of how quickly things change.

I have never let myself feel too proud or smug that you guys are sleeping through the night because, as all parents know, as soon as I do it'll all go out of the window. A sickness bug, teething, nightmares,

thunderstorms, bedwetting, thirst, a missing toy –
there are many things that can throw a spanner in the
works and push everything off balance.

I know some people aren't fond of children
crawling into their parents' beds at night, but I have to
say that I absolutely love it as you clamber in and get
under the duvet. I love the fact that you've woken up
and want to have us close. I'd rather pick you up and
plonk you between us than have you unsettled in the
middle of the night and us unable to comfort you (like
when Buddy has night terrors). There's no trauma, no
anxiety, just all of us sleeping like we're the Waltons,
or the grandparents in *Charlie and the Chocolate Factory*.
There'll come a point when you no longer want to do
this so I'm enjoying it while I can – especially on
nights when your dad is away and there's even more
space in the bed.

Coming out of our snoozes injects adrenalin into
my day from the off. Pre-kids, I thought mornings
would be a thing of beauty, us all waking up with a
yawn and a stretch, taking in the day before shuffling
into one bed for a snuggle and a giggle under crisp
white sheets and thinking about how lucky we all are.

The reality is that I actually jump out of bed and
rush frantically to the child who's calling to soothe/

shush/comfort them before they wake everyone else up. Either that or I'm woken by the sound of thudding feet crossing the landing and heading towards me. As soon as the face reaches mine and notices I'm awake I know I have to start negotiating enough time to collect my bra before you run out of the room and call me to take you downstairs. It's a mad dash. No time for lingering, no time for stretching – and I definitely have zero time for crisp white sheets: they're not even ironed.

Big love,
Mumma xx

Dear Buzz,

You fell over tonight – and, yes, one of your knees did wallop the floor but your scream was so dramatic that your dad and I both rushed over to you.

My heart was racing as I scooped you into my arms, expecting to find a broken leg or a pool of blood.

There was nothing but a slightly pink splodge of unbroken skin. Yes, it looked sore, but it didn't require a trip to A and E – it didn't even need a plaster!

I should've known the whole thing wasn't as bad as I'd feared. The Scream is your standard response to everything at the moment – mostly Buddy taking a toy from you, or you two having a squabble.

With you still in my arms, I decided to take the moment to talk about our reactions and how they don't have to be so big if we aren't actually in pain.

You were still wailing.

Wailing loudly.

Then you suddenly stopped, as though you seemed to take stock of your injuries and were surprised with what you found.

'My mouth is crying, but my eyes are dry.' You smiled, realizing you were fine.

I couldn't help but giggle at the jump from inconsolable despair to giddy joy, as that pretty much sums you up right now. You give everything your all – especially when it comes to emotion.

I remember being shouted at when I hurt myself or momentarily got lost when I was younger and I get it now: as a parent there's that cocktail of fear and relief and you don't know which emotion to let out first. Your heart is pumping loudly and there is an enormous release of adrenalin as your body prepares to fight for you. Well, I always will, my little crumb.

Love you!
Mumma xx

I'M SO GLAD IT'S YOU!

Dear Tom,

Almost six years ago we walked into the hospital as a duo knowing that our lives were about to change for ever. We even took a photo of the pair of us on the walk from the car to the hospital, with our wedding venue in the background.
We weren't silly.
We knew there was
a huge shift coming
and wanted to
document the last
moment of it being
just us. Did you think
the shift would play
out in quite this way,
though?

Back when we were kids we'd meet up on the school stairs, mulling over our 'problems', like we were in a scene from *Dawson's Creek*, before spending the remainder of our lunchtime kissing. At the start of our twenties we moved into the home we're still in, bringing along the fun and chaos of endless house parties and celebrations. We were never big clubbers or partygoers out of the house, it always seemed too much of a faff, and the comfort of being at home hidden from prying eyes kept us there. To us, going to our local with the guys and going home for a dance where we'd throw the most ridiculous moves was far more appealing than being somewhere we'd all be watched and judged. We weren't cool and we didn't care. We just loved each other's company and letting loose.

One a.m. was our bedtime, 10 a.m. an early morning.

We went on a last-minute trip to LA just to see John Williams play at the Superbowl without having to worry about childcare. We jumped around Disney World without having to worry about stroller-parking or nap-times. We cycled around Paris looking for the Rose Line mentioned in Dan Brown's *The Da Vinci Code* without having to keep little ones entertained.

For years it was just us, and as a result we entered into parenthood as a solid couple.

We are not perfect, and some days are more testing than others, but I think we balance each other out. We take it in turns to be the nutty one barking orders, and then the one taking the calmer approach. Doing so helps me learn so much. If you were always the measured one, I would feel so inadequate and inept.

On the days when I've struggled, you've been there. It's not even like you have to say or do anything specific, but you know our children and love them as much as I do, and you also know how they can

play up. You don't even need to hear it sometimes, you
just have to tell me they've been like that for you
too – or just come in with your fresh, serene energy
and take over, instinctively knowing that's what
the room needs and aware of the buttons being
pushed.

We are currently both shattered, as one would
expect with three boys and our inability to get to bed
early in the evenings, even though we know we'll
probably be up in the night and definitely be up by
6 a.m. The difficulty is our workload, and trying to
utilize the time when the kids are asleep to get some
of it done. Of course we could chill out on the sofa
but as we both juggle being there for our children all
day, we see the evening as guilt-free work time. There
is no need to feel like a bad parent when we're
working those hours, because our little loves are in the
Land of Nod and don't need us.

I guess the thing we have to start striking more of a
balance on, though, is *us*. You and me. Currently we
work until about ten, then congregate on the sofa for
a little treat and an episode of something lighthearted
and fun while our bodies lean in. This is our time to
switch off.

I think we both need that time to have something

just wash over us without requiring too much from our brains . . . although perhaps we should stop popping the TV on and just chat – when do we get a chance to sit together and do that uninterrupted now?

Remember when we were teenagers and we'd be on the phone to each other every night after school? We'd sit there for hours, only saying goodbye when one of our mums came on the phone (no doubt listening in from another room) to tell us to get off. What did we find so fascinating to talk about? How did the conversation not dry up? I remember being very happy sitting in silence and smiling into the receiver: we just liked being linked.

Now life is more serious. Problems are bigger. Knock-on effects of decisions are greater – but the discussions around them are shorter, or put off somehow until we're in the right headspace.

We need more time for us. More time for me to make you laugh, for me to enjoy the brilliant person you are. More time to be the couple who walked through those hospital doors all those years ago. Yes, we've changed, but our love for and devotion to each other haven't – we just need to make time to show it.

Funnily enough, I've always cited family time as

our time. I thought being out with our family, the little humans we created who are a little bit of you and a little bit of me, was the greatest way for us to be together and show each other love. And we do find those moments where everyone is happy, laughing and content, causing us to glance at each other with pride and admiration. Yet they're not the same.

It's difficult to fully immerse ourselves in the love we feel for one another for a substantial amount of time when we're chasing kids around the park on their bikes, weighed down with discarded scooters and helmets, or trying to get the boys to sit at a table in a restaurant.

When we're out as a family, or even at home with them, they require so much of our energy that we don't get the time to connect properly like we used to. We get the leftover bits. We can become snappy with each other. There's other stuff going on, and that contributes to the mental load, which can make it all feel overwhelming.

Something is telling me we need to set aside some time for us. Whether that's taking work out of the equation at weekends and having a later dinner together, just the two of us, or ensuring we get out for a date night once a month.

My point is that I don't want to give you my leftovers any more. We both deserve more than the scraps that decide to stick stubbornly to the plate at the end of a busy day. We're lucky that we've never had any problems in our marriage – no massive arguments, no dramas, no walking out or looking elsewhere – but we do need to make sure we don't take what we have for granted.

So, from me to you, I just want to say that I'm all in. I need you, I need us, and I'm so glad to have you as my co-pilot in this crazy world. There is no one else I would rather navigate my way through parenthood with. Honestly. No one.

My love is yours,
Love,
The old ball and chain
'Er indoors
Poopoohead Mumma
Giovanna
Your wife xxx

Dear Boys,

This weekend we left all three of you for the first time – for two whole nights! That's forty-eight hours of us being out of parent mode and you being looked after by someone else. Your Nonno, my dad, arrived at midday on Friday with Nonna, and we got into the car with Aunty Giorgie and Uncle Chickpea (Summer Rae has also been with you all weekend) to drive to Somerset for our closest friends' Katy and Yusuf's wedding.

I was pretty anxious before we left. The week leading up to it I worried

243

how Nonno would get on with four children. You are
a month into summer holidays, have all had
chickenpox and now seem to have more energy and
fight in you than ever. You do not stop from morning
to night. You love each other and play alongside each
other beautifully some of the time, then suddenly
break out into a brawl, with punches and kicks being
thrown in rage. Seriously, Katy and Yusuf came over
the other night and it was carnage. Granted it was
witching hour, and having people turn up at that time
tends to send you all into overdrive, *but* it was a lot.
You were a lot – even if there were moments you were
adorable with the face paints (which then got rubbed
on to the yellow sofa). You simply wouldn't listen to a
thing I said and were relentless. If I, your mother, was
reduced to tears (I felt totally out of control), what
would you do to Nonno?

But when I phoned him his response was 'They're
kids.' His plan was to let you all do what you wanted
(to a degree) and just go with it . . . He's fairly chilled
out and happy to go with the flow and also loves
playing with you, so I let his words comfort me a bit.
Although you can be challenging, you are just kids. I
guess the joy for you of Nonno and Nonna coming in
for the weekend is that the focus would be all on you

guys, not split between anything else your dad and I would typically get distracted with – like work or household chores.

Friday morning, the day we were setting off, Max woke up with a temperature and was a bit under the weather. I was gutted that I wasn't leaving three happy kids who were in fine form and just prayed things would run as smoothly as possible for your grandparents.

It was a frantic morning, mostly because I'd been so consumed with getting everything sorted for you guys that we'd left our packing to the last minute. That said, when we were finally in the car the anxiety I'd been feeling started to fade. We were off. There was no going back now. I wanted to make the most of the weekend and couldn't wait to see the kindest, most thoughtful and caring woman I know get married to a brilliant man. I was going to be having fun with people who've known me for over sixteen years, people who have watched me grow up and seen me at my worst and best. It was time to get away and immerse myself in good natter, dancing and soul-feeding joy.

I decided to share a picture of the milk in the fridge, with a little caption about going away to watch my best friend get married. It was fun, light, and captured the love in my heart for motherhood and the excitement of seeing my bestie wed. The response from people online was lovely, yet there was one mum who posted to tell me how damaging it would be for Max, a breastfed baby, to be away from me for that length of time – all done so I could 'just get drunk with mates' . . . Oh, my heart. The anxiety crept up my skin, like a spider looking for somewhere to spin its web and set up its home. My happiness wavered.

I wasn't just looking for an excuse to get drunk with my mates: it was an important and special wedding. It was two nights because it was five hours away. You boys weren't left with strangers but with people who loved you . . . but that one negative comment caused me to doubt that I was doing the right thing. I found myself wondering if I could have done anything differently. Then I went back to the post and saw the comments made in relation to that one. They were all from people who saw the words as judgemental, unnecessary and wrong, people being supportive and kind. I decided to message back to defuse the situation: someone had scrolled back through the original person's feed to find hashtags on her own timeline about spending time away from her

baby. I didn't want things to get personal or for one person's throwaway comment to cause any more hurt than it already had. I was nice, reassured her that my children were well looked after with people who loved them, then sent her a bit of love and commented on how tough this parenting malarkey is. I don't know why that mum felt the need to bring down my mood, but I didn't want people bashing her for it. I don't know what was going through her mind, or where she was at mentally. We all have wobbles, and it's easy to hit out at someone you see only on the internet. Kindness is something I feel we should offer wherever we can.

Her comment started a chain of people detailing their first time away from their children. They also reminded me that Max is almost a year old, and not as needy as he was eleven months ago. Aside from that, they reassured me that time away from being mum is a good thing, and important.

Getting there on the Friday night and sitting with my mates around the campfire was magical. I was no longer Mum, and although a lot of conversations were about you three, or motherhood, it was great to reclaim a bit more of me. I didn't think I missed the old me, and I know I've said I don't think about losing my identity, but that weekend made me see that old me and new me are all me, and that both versions can still exist without taking away the shine of the other.

Just because I was child-free for the weekend didn't mean I was getting so drunk I was spewing into bushes, but I went for a run with your dad in the morning, enjoyed being a part of the ceremony, then loved dancing and laughing with my mates while having a tipple. All that, without feeling I needed to make sure you were safe or had to keep a clear head so that I could take care of you. My attention wasn't split – which could also be down to the fact there was little phone signal so I could just immerse myself in the moment rather than feeling torn.

I danced so much my knees started to swell. I laughed so much the back of my head started to ache. I felt so proud of my gorgeous friends and the love in the air that my insides were set to burst. All this happened without you there. All this happened and it did not lessen my love for you. It did not take away the fact that you three boys are the anchor of my heart.

Yes, I missed you, but I also had a jolly good time shouting along to the music and jumping around on the dance floor without a care in the world. It felt wonderful being just me and not having to be the responsible one, and it made me incredibly happy to look at your dad and see him have fun too.

Not one single part of me would wish parenthood away, and I know how lucky we are to be your parents, but the weekend showed me that if we want you to have the happiest of upbringings and be brought up in a loving home, then we need time to cool off, shake it all out, then come back to you as a unified couple who are reminded of how good we can make each other feel, even with a look.

So, on this journey home (I'm not in the slightest hung-over – but your dad isn't looking his best), I'm thinking about how good it'll be to see you all, but my heart is also lighter for my having grasped the importance of time away. I'm not slinking off to live the life I lived before, wishing I was free of you, or remembering the old me with longing and sorrow. No. It's simply to get some respite from the mental load and to ensure I can give you the best of me.

I love you so much and can't wait to squish you when I'm back with you!

Love,
Mumma xx

PS We got home to chaos in the playroom, a handful of broken toys, and a derailed door *but* you were all happy to see us – especially Nonno and Nonna, who had been run ragged. They did, however, offer to do it again. Hurrah!

MY DAD, MY VERY OWN YODA

Dear Dad,

You have always had wise words to offer us kids, especially when we hit our teens. Sometimes you'll be quite cryptic with your advice, leaving us to sit and ponder over your actual feelings. When we were younger, we'd ask to go out or stay at a friend's house. Mum would tell us to 'ask your dad', and you'd throw the decision back our way, like Yoda testing us on our chosen path. (Who'd have thought? A *Star Wars* reference. I'd never watched a single film until I met Tom. The Fletchers have changed me!) I'd always read into your reply far deeper than I should have, but I wanted to please you and make you happy. I always have.

You've always been a wise one, but there were certain moments that really resonated with me, which I know will have an effect on how I mother my children in the future. One such moment occurred when I was around thirteen and was emptying the dishwasher. We'd just started using some of your wedding china – you had two sets (to my knowledge). One was cream with a beautiful delicate floral design, the other white and brown and fairly ugly (I took the ugly set away with me to Sidcup when I left home, and we used it until we got fresh crockery as a wedding present). Anyway, both sets were rarely used, stored up high in the cupboard, and we needed to stand on one of the kitchen bar stools to reach them.

On that particular occasion, as I clambered up on to the stool, I put my hand on a shelf to pull myself up. Big mistake. Huge. The shelf tipped forwards, sending the whole floral crockery set flying forwards to crash to the tiles below. I was shit scared, mortified and tearful all at once.

You came running in and I prepared myself for a bollocking. You took one look at the mess and said, 'Well, now you don't have to put it away.' It was your way of reassuring me, and I've never forgotten it. Looking back, I realize it must've given you quite the fright too, and that you probably thought something had happened to one of us when you first heard the commotion. I now recognize the feeling of relief you would've felt at seeing your child, me, unharmed when you feared the worst. A smashed piece of china, a broken chair or shattered vase is nothing. Items are either replaceable or, more often than not, possible to live without. You can't say the same for your children.

This sentiment was repeated again when I was eighteen years old, and you had a similar reaction when I smashed into our brick wall in the car you'd bought me. I'd *just* passed my driving test and my boyfriend at the time was grinning at me from the driveway. I wasn't paying attention and, trying to

impress him, cut the corner too sharply. The car caught on the wall causing a huge scraping sound. I didn't know what to do. I was stuck. Mum came rushing out to help, but I was horrified at what I'd done to the car – not to mention embarrassed that my boyfriend had seen me do something so idiotic. I'd been looking quite cool until that point.

When I got free, I found the car door had gained scratches and a dent. Thankfully the wall was unharmed, but I had to phone you to tell you what I'd done to the car you'd forked out on. 'The car is just a car. The important thing is that you're OK,' was your reply.

Thank heavens for that!

You knew I wouldn't have meant to steer the car into the wall like that, and the shock was enough to make me take more care from then on when I was pulling on to the drive. Sometimes it's not worth harping on about an act that can't be undone . . . right?

I've heard people say that they grew up with nothing, and that's why they get upset when stuff gets broken or wears out. I find it fascinating that a man who grew up in the mountains of Italy and didn't have much in the way of possessions can brush off things like this so easily. Especially when you came over here with two suitcases – one with clothes, the other with pasta and tomato sauce (a fact that will never fail to put a smile on my face) – and have worked your butt off for everything you have. But I guess that's the point. You worked hard to make money for your family. You are not materialistic because you have lived without and know what joy can be found in not-having.

I don't know. Maybe I'm over-thinking you, and you were just being laidback in those moments while you were quietly seething inside, but I don't think so.

The other important piece of advice you gave me growing up came when I started learning to drive. 'Remember, everyone else is out to kill you.' It wasn't necessarily my own driving that I needed to worry about, but other people's. I've never forgotten it . . . I would say that has made me a more careful driver, but Tom might disagree. ;-)

Dad, I can't wait to see what pieces of wisdom you impart to my boys. You're unpredictable, caring and patient – and always ready for an adventure. I have no doubt we'll all go on many.

Love you,
One of your favourite daughters xx

To the Oxo Mum,

Before becoming a mum I had visions of what I would look like in that matriarchal role. I would be a cross between Maria from *The Sound of Music* and you. I grew up with your adverts. Through the years, your 'family' lightheartedly showed the challenges of family life while you all sat and tucked into a meal (which invariably included a good smothering of gravy spooned over it).

Your food kept your loved ones coming back for more: no matter what was going on in their lives, you were there with a hot meal to bring everyone together and provide comfort and warmth.

You were one of my motherhood idols, and for years I've been saying how I wanted to be more like you but thought I'd failed . . . But tonight, as a mother, I went back and watched those adverts again, wondering if I'd view them differently now.

Oh, how I wept.

They are not what I thought they were. Yes, they do show a family sitting around the table at dinner time, but they also show the chaos, the noise, the confrontation, the love and the heartache of family life. They highlight the push and pull between wanting everything to be perfect and accepting life for exactly what it is. Honestly, the last advert you made where you're sitting in your kitchen for the final time had me in bits.

In my effort to be more you, and recognizing that mealtimes are something I really care about, we eat as a family as much as we possibly can. Breakfast and dinner are the main meals we tuck into together, all eating the same meal at the same time.

My boys love their food.

Mealtimes generally start off well, but can descend into chaos from the off as Buzz and Buddy decide who should sit where and on what colour chair. Next up there could be a dispute over cutlery and whether

they want a children's set or an adult fork. Then the plates can be rejected – the wrong picture on a plastic one or they may want an adult's side plate so that they feel more grown-up. Then there could be faffing over water cups . . .

When the dinner is finally placed on the table there is a moment of stillness. Sometimes, depending on their mood, I hold my breath in anticipation of what's to come next. Are they going to moan and reject the food we've cooked without tasting it? Or will they get stuck in, munching away while having a natter?

Thankfully, it's generally the latter. In that moment I feel euphoric – because I am most like you, my table looking like yours did in those adverts, my children semi-interested in what I've made.

However, my euphoria usually lasts for no more than two minutes before someone is out of their seat, sometimes running to the loo, or doing laps of the table, like they're racing in Formula 1, or maybe just fidgeting in their chair before sliding off it and causing mayhem under the table.

I know this is not how they behave at school or elsewhere, but it seems to be the standard approach at home once they've eaten enough to take the edge off their hunger. They get each other excited – and if friends or relatives are with us, *forget it*!

You'd be right to wonder what I do in such a situation. Do I shout? Do I order them back to the table and tell them they need to finish their dinner? Do I go along with their games and then bring them back to the table nicely? Do I block it all out and get on with mine while I can?

I mean, it totally depends on how hungry I am and how long it's taken to cook the blooming dinner!

I have to say, Oxo Mum, this has led to many a stressful dinner time but it is very, very, very slowly getting better. The novelty of being able to get up and out of their seats is starting to wane ever so slightly, and I'm hopeful that the older two will be glued to their chairs by the time Max ventures out of his high-chair and gets the ball rolling again.

Despite all this disruption, I still love mealtimes. All right, I'm not the biggest fan of taking the boys to restaurants right now – I'd much rather have them at

home in a controlled (and contained) environment – but that'll change soon enough.

One day I might find myself sitting in my kitchen on my own, reflecting on the good times we had in there when the boys were little, and all the meals we've shared. There'll be the thought of Buzz eating like a rabbit, the image of Buddy dancing while wearing his pants on his head, then the joy on Max's face as he sprays milk from his lips and it covers everything within a two-metre radius . . . all of this will make me weep with joy.

That table in our home is the core of our family life and, although the time spent around it can be wild and berserk, I blooming love it.

Thank you for showing its importance and being an inspiration!

Giovanna xx

PS Although I really don't know what you were thinking when you put gravy on the meatballs! MADNESS! ;-)

Dear Tom,

One day they *might* all leave home, and then it'll be just you and me again. Can you imagine the quiet that'll descend upon us, and how deserted the house will seem? The fridge will be empty with just the two of us to cook for. There'll be no need to fill it. And we won't have to buy three bunches of bananas a week for fear of running out!

Do you think the boys, our men, will want to come back for Sunday lunch? Or do you think they'll fly the nest and rarely even call? Do you think they'll still want us actively involved and around when given the choice? Or do you think they'll abandon us for their significant others?

Gosh, you know me, I'm getting teary now, even though this is well over a decade away.

The thought of them leaving, and this intensive phase of parenting being over, is so overwhelming. They'll no longer be dependent on us for everything. They probably won't value our advice or seek our company . . . What if they phase us out? Ha! As if! They'll definitely be back for the Disney trips, if nothing else!

What do you imagine we'll do with all our free time? Will we live differently when we don't have to be there physically for them every day? Will we go travelling and see more of the world? Will we rest? Will we enjoy the lazy mornings we can finally indulge in or will we be waking up at the crack of dawn, the 5 a.m. starts hardwired in our body clocks after enduring years of sudden yelps from our human alarm clocks?

Will we reconnect in a new way? Remember what life was like before and marvel at how familiar it feels, even though we've been through so much and changed so massively since the last time we lived alone?

Will we drink more in the evenings when we no longer have to be responsible? Or will we go out

running for longer? Will we run together when one of us no longer has to stay with the children? Will we try new things? Join clubs? Find new hobbies? New things to stress over? Will we feel lighter or more anxious? Will we move abroad, or down the road from wherever Buzz, Buddy and Max end up? Or will we continuously find reasons to drop in on them as we're casually 'driving past' even if they've moved to the other side of London, or the world?

Will we be lonely?

Will we miss them? Will we long for the chaos we're currently living in?

Will we like each other still?

Will I be enough?

Honey, do you think we're doing a good job? Isn't that the question every parent asks themselves, and keeps asking themselves even when their children are fully fledged adults? I knew about the guilt I would feel as a mum, but there's also a weight that I don't think will ever lift. Do you think our parents feel that? Do *you*?

I'm apprehensive over what life might do to them. I ache over the heartbreak they'll one day have to face. I hurt, knowing I won't be able to wrap them up in cotton wool and keep them safe from life's challenges and obstacles, or be able to guide them at every step like we have so far.

We gave them life, but life can be so cruel, it makes my heart feel heavy.

I just hope we do enough, that we *are* enough, and that we can continue to provide them with the right tools to see them through whatever life chucks their way. I hope we give them enough guidance and love, yet freedom and independence.

Quite frankly, I hope we don't f**k them up, and that when the time comes for them to be more independent, they are ready.

A month in Bali followed by months in Australia, New Zealand, South America and Hawaii does sound lovely, though . . .

Here's to not losing each other on the way there (said while holding an imaginary piña colada in my hand and raising it into the air).

Love you,
   Giovanna xx

PS I mean, all this is hypothetical. We both know Buzz is never leaving. ;-)

DINNER DATE FOR THREE . . .

Dear Buddy,

Your dad and I decided to set time aside tonight and have a takeaway once you boys were in bed. We probably do this once a month, followed by a film, as it forces us to have a whole night away from our desks and spend some properly dedicated time together.

We'd had an active day of bike rides and bowling, so we imagined you'd be asleep as soon as your heads hit the pillows. That was certainly the case for Buzz and Max, but you lay there with your eyes wide open, just turning every now and then to make sure your daddy was still in the

room. You were almost asleep ten minutes later when our gate buzzer went off: our takeaway had arrived.

By this point you were wide awake. Your dad tried to get you to go to sleep before he came down to have his dinner, but you would just appear on the stairs seconds later. You weren't crying or kicking up a fuss, just intrigued to see what we were up to.

Some chatting and reasoning later, you agreed to stay in bed while we had our dinner. I started dishing up while your dad popped to the loo . . . and there you were, sitting on the stairs with your chin cupped in your hands, looking all cute and adorable.

You know I can't resist you when you're sitting like that.

I caved in, deciding it would be easier to have you with us for a bit rather than running up and down the stairs while I was trying to eat. At least that way we'd still be able to enjoy the food hot. You had the biggest of grins on your face at being allowed to join us.

You did not stop talking, telling us all about your adventures, the leaves in the garden and how you cook them in your mud kitchen, about the rainbow birthday cake you would like (in six months' time) with animals on top, about how prawn crackers make cookies when mixed with apples, and about how your nails grow . . . The topics were varied and we just let you talk while we ate. We were lost in your chattiness while realizing you never get a chance to be with us and have our full attention. I'm so glad we brought you downstairs, and I promise we'll start giving you more of our time for you to have all to yourself.

Tonight might not have been what we planned – we didn't get to watch *End Game* – but it was perfect having you with us, sharing your brilliance, reminding us that, even though sometimes it's tough and we feel

we're getting it all wrong, we're actually doing all right. Because just look at you!

Love you, Bubba, Your Mumma xx

To all the mums and dads
(but especially the mums who find
it hard to switch off),

We've been away to the countryside this weekend. We went with friends but there was no plan other than to be together and eat.

'What's the plan Gi?' someone asked, within the first hour of our getting there.

Fuck.

No plan.

Nothing.

I had a moment of self-doubt. I'd brought everyone away to somewhere remote in the countryside but hadn't made us a schedule. I hadn't thought through the games we could play, the walks we could go on, or the places nearby we could visit. I'd love to say this in itself was the plan, the plan being to have no plan, but there really was no plan because I hadn't had time to think about making one. I only had time to focus on the destination and getting us there around nap-times.

The idea of having nothing to do is a scary one.

We're so used to scrolling through Instagram and seeing other families having fun days out and doing things that we feel we're failing if we're not doing the same. We're so riddled with guilt for being away and working that we feel we have to fill the days we spend with our children doing things and taking them to exciting places. We're so used to trying to juggle everything and squeezing all we can out of a day that standing still is alien. The thought of being unproductive and having nothing to show at the end of a day for what we've been doing leads us to feel lazy, guilty and on edge.

Wasted time.

There's a feeling we should be doing something, organizing or preparing. So, stopping and just being, stopping and just immersing yourself in a game with your children – IT FEELS WEIRD! It feels like we're not doing the things we should be, even though in that moment we're exactly where we're meant to be.

The thing is, they'll remember you playing Bulldog far more than they will the roast you spent hours preparing (so you could sit and watch them moan about it), the clean clothes you've put them in (which'll quickly get mucky), or that you spent hours tidying up their clothes, toys and the general whirlwind of mess that follows in their wake (although they will wonder where you put the obscure yellow brick that is now their most treasured possession and will lead to huge meltdowns if not found).

Obviously all the stuff we do in keeping them clean, fed and clothed is important, but when I remember

what I thought motherhood would be like before I
became a mum, I didn't think of the endless list of
chores and things to organize. The visions in my head
were of being with my children. Of giving them
cuddles on the sofa, all cosy under blankets while we
watched a film on a cold wintry afternoon. I saw us
enjoying lazy mornings in bed where everyone
bundles in and we all eat buttery toast and slurp milk.
I saw us running along beaches, playing games in the
garden, going for long walks in the country, spending
hours together creating bits and bobs with our arts
and crafts kits, and laughing around the dinner table
while my children shared the silliest of jokes.

I saw us having fun.

OK, this was the ideal, and I know my role is
harder and more complex than I thought it would be.
Children don't comply with the fun or sentimental
moments we want to create – as soon as they wake us
up my kids want to go downstairs rather than get
under the duvet with me. Lounging in bed is boring
to them. Neither do they want me to force them into
sitting down and quietly making a beautiful card –
things like that happen only on their terms and, as a
creative person, that's something I fully understand.
Also, right now, their jokes aren't that funny, but

they're learning, and the things they like to do with me will change. I just have to be there for the moments they want me.

Life isn't what I thought it would be, but it's so easy to get caught up in the organizational side that we forget to enjoy the bits that made us want to have kids in the first place. After all, I didn't become a mum to pair up socks!

I think I'm on a bit of a learning curve. Sometimes motherhood isn't much fun because I'm trying to cram so much in. But doing nothing is doing something. Because doing nothing means not worrying about anything other than being together and seeing what happens. It means not going off (just yet) to cook dinner, not deciding to get everyone to tidy up their toys and help unload the table. It means playing Chicken, Hero Twin, with all your focus, determination and joy, and seeing your children crack up laughing as they chase you across the garden.

Do nothing more.

Love,
Giovanna xx

Dear Me,

It is not selfish to take time for yourself.

I know, I know. This goes against everything you've ever been taught. Putting yourself first is ugly and self-centred: you're meant to put others first and make sure they're happy, loved and cared for before you consider taking time for yourself. But if you're always putting others first, who is doing the same for you? People in your life care deeply for you and help you along, but that duty falls mostly on you. So why does the idea of 'self-care' leave some of us feeling a bit queasy?

I'm sure it's the ruddy mum-guilt rearing its awful head again. If you're not with your children how could you possibly spend that time doing anything but work or useful things around the house? Surely getting your hair done, going for a massage or having lunch with a mate is nothing but self-indulgent and neglectful.

Isn't it?

Time is tight, and trying to squeeze in something for yourself might feel like one more thing to add to a never-ending to-do list. It's the first thing that can be erased or overlooked, or you simply forget to clear some space for it in the diary – but at what point is that a terrible idea? When you're not sleeping properly because you have no time to zone out of the mental load? When you're constantly anxious? When you stop absorbing the wonder of life because you've got lost in all the shit on your plate? When you run yourself into a nervous breakdown and can't get out of bed?

Well, that doesn't sound like a very good plan.

Maybe a little bit of time to catch your breath is a better idea.

At an event recently Jess Jones, known online as The Fat Funny One, said that instead of self-care she refers to it as self-compassion. Essentially, we have to be kinder to ourselves rather than constantly feeling guilty, worthless and as if we're failing when we're actually doing a good job. We have to give ourselves the respect we deserve before expecting others to send it our way. We have to know when it's time to stop and pour some TLC into ourselves – because, it turns out, you can't pour anything from an empty jug!

Well, I'm ready to show you some compassion and make sure you're strong, able and full to the brim with radiance and wonder. There won't always be time to have thirty minutes out running, but I will take a minute or two to breathe and feel a bit of stillness and calm – even if that time is snatched while I'm breathing in my morning coffee. I'll stop and be in that moment, willing the caffeine to give me an extra kick of energy for the day ahead.

You have to take the time to unwind from everyone else's day-to-day requirements. You need to keep connecting with friends, and remember to laugh with family. Being a mum requires so much from you, yet you've already failed if you start from a place of having nothing left to give. Look after your mind! Your mental health is so incredibly important that you should do all you can to look after what is going into it. Don't get sucked into comparisons, labels or opinions.

Do you.

Motherhood is crazy, and you're right to find it difficult, to question yourself and to get things wrong. Accept that your buttons will be pressed and that you will feel lost as a result. You are not perfect and you have to forgive yourself for not blooming being the Oxo Mum or Maria from *The Sound of Music* . . . Not only were they fictional characters, but the simple fact is that short hair wouldn't suit you anyway. Leave your matriarchal pin-ups at the door.

You do not have to spend a lifetime wishing you were a different type of mother, more connected, more capable: you just have to do your version and focus on your bond with your children. They don't care that Susie's mum makes their chicken nuggets from scratch while yours come out of the freezer, that Jake's mum folds his pants rather than stuffing them into a drawer, or that Barry's mum buys him organic raspberries from the supermarket while your boys pick them from a bush while out for a walk (sounds idyllic but they've probably been peed on). You don't get extra mum points for that stuff. You really don't. So, leave the judgement at the door, along with Oxo and Maria. That pressure, that doubt, that sense of being unworthy will do you no good. I promise you!

I know at times being a mum makes you question your very existence and sanity, but you're at the helm of your little empire, so go conquer and shape it in a way that suits the whole family.

You've got this. Really. And I have to say (on the whole) you're doing a great job! (Almost) the best.

Love,
Me. You. Oh, bugger, I'm getting myself confused now. Xxxxx

Dear Boys,

You didn't come with us to see
our friends Katy and Yusuf
(Yufus to you) get married so
we said we'd throw a party
especially for you so that you
could celebrate too. So today
Katy and Yusuf came over and
we decided to redo the wedding
for you three, Phoebe and Oscar.
Katy got into my bridesmaid dress
(handily white), Charlie picked
flowers from the garden for a
bouquet, a Fisher-Price doorframe
was used as the altar, an aisle was
made with the multi-coloured

281

children's chairs, and we used red lentils instead of
confetti. I was on hand as the unofficial celebrant and
your dad was the self-appointed unofficial
photographer.

'Here Comes the Bride' started playing as Katy
walked through the garden, and the beams on your
faces were adorable. You remained transfixed as Katy
and Yusuf declared their love for each other (through
fits of giggles) and pinky-promised to love each other
always. Romance and magic filled the air. I saw them
dancing in your eyes as you took it all in, swept up by
the enchanting scene.

Buzz wasn't too impressed with the kiss at the end
(he thought it was gross), but it was a gorgeous few
minutes, and really reminded me of the mock
wedding ceremonies we used to have at school. Even
at nine years old we knew marriage was a serious
affair, not to be taken lightly or thoughtlessly. I
remember on one occasion someone even made a cake
for afterwards and another had 'designed' the veil,
made of loo roll we'd snuck out of the toilets! It was a
real party of love as we innocently pulled together to
make the union between our peers happen!

As I sit here tonight looking through the photos
your dad took and reflecting on what you made of the

whole thing, I wonder about the love you'll experience
throughout your lives – the love beyond our family.
The kind you'll gain from a significant other, whom
you'll want to dote on and care for. Will you marry
someone at school? Come home and declare you have
to make a cake for the event or (and this happened
with the boy who proposed when I was eight years
old) pinch all my rings and hand them to the one you
love? Will you love fleetingly or deeply? Will you
hanker or move on? Will you experience the pain of
unrequited love or the torture of forbidden love,
which causes your heart to deepen its emotions in the

most painful of ways? Will you open your heart and chuck out the love in spades? Or will you be measured and reserved, only giving your love when it has been earned? Will you be cuddly and affectionate or rely on words to convey your intentions? Will you let people in or will you hold up barriers for others to try to break down?

Will you get hurt?

Oh, gosh . . . Of course you'll get hurt. Love is the most encompassing thing you'll ever experience. It takes over every inch of your being, every cell in your body. When all of you is so intrinsically invested, it's naïve to imagine you won't feel pain if love lets you down.

And it will.

Love will guide you through the toughest of times, but it'll also cause them. The depth of your commitment and devotion will undoubtedly cause you the most pain if it is ever lost, damaged or misplaced.

Hearing that, you might think that being without love seems like the easiest option – but a lack of love is black and dark. It's empty and void of life. I don't believe you can live without the hope, joy and fulfilment that comes with love. If they have nothing

else but love I believe a person can be happy, no matter what. Love will be there to offer comfort and guidance. Without love, *any* love, that's too bleak an existence for me.

Love may be hidden from time to time, and we can be left feeling lonely and isolated, but love is always there in some capacity.

You're probably wondering what I'm waffling on about now. My point is that love is the greatest gift. Give it completely, and be careful when you're lucky enough to receive it. Treat it with respect and loyalty. Don't take it for granted, or clamp it so tightly that it feels suffocated and unable to grow. Tend it, nurture it, and be so very proud of how that love blossoms.

To receive someone's heart is the greatest of all gifts.

Love you,
Mumma xx

THE FAMILY PICTURE

To the ones who claim my sons' hearts . . .

Welcome to the family. Have we met yet? Does he
talk about us? Is he worried to bring you home?
Maybe he's embarrassed by us in some way, or
you're nervous of
meeting his folks. Maybe
you're super-keen to
come over. Maybe he
thinks it's too soon. Or is
it the other way around?

Sorry.

I'm sticking my nose
where I shouldn't.

I just get excited when I
think of the people who will
be entering our lives via my

sons' hearts. Excited and apprehensive. It makes me want to weep a bit – because I worship them and the thought of them being all grown-up and in love with someone, making a real connection with a significant other, fills me with so much emotion.

You will replace us. Literally. Right now when the boys are asked to draw pictures of their family, it's us – Tom, me, Buzz, Buddy and Max (the cats if they're lucky). We are their family. We are their inner circle.

One day you will claim their hearts, go on to get married, have kids – or maybe even without those things, you will be their family.

As a result of that shift we will become the outer circle, always there but set a little further apart from them.

When he talks of his immediate family, it won't be us he means.

If you have kids they'll draw their family picture of themselves with you and my sons but we won't be sketched. It won't even cross their minds to add us.

Please don't get me wrong, that's exactly the way it should be. I should not be in that drawing. It's not my place to be in it. Not really. My role will have changed and I will always be there for you all but I will have stepped to the left so I can leave the frame. But it's

OK. Rather than having a leading role in the story, I'll have become a supporting actress.

Years ago I remember sitting at a family meal with Tom's grandparents, Joan and Ken. Their three daughters were there with their husbands, as were all the grandchildren, partners and great-grandchildren. We'd come together in a local restaurant to celebrate their wedding anniversary, and as we were sitting there, an overwhelming wave of emotion swept over me (I was probably pregnant at the time). Joan and Ken had started off as two separate people but, through their love for one another, their family had grown and now all those people celebrating there were a part of it, and it is still growing. I felt so in awe of the power of a family tree and its roots in those two wonderful people.

One day Tom and I will be looking proudly at our sons, our grandchildren, and at you.

It's hard to think of myself as a mother-in-law. I love mine but there are so many jokes about mums-in-law interfering and being overbearing, rude, possessive and cold – and I don't want to get it wrong.

A little part of me will always see my children as my babies, as the little loves I brought into the world. Whom I nursed and rocked to sleep. Whom I bathed and fed. Whom I cheered on as they learnt to crawl, then walk and run. Whom I repeatedly said, 'Mumma,' to in the hope they'd ask for me before Tom. Whom I laughed with and chatted to. Whom I would pick up when they cried, and weep for when they were hurt. They will always be the ones I labelled 'my everything' – because it took so much of me to raise them.

Those babies made me the person I am today, and I am so happy and grateful for their existence. But, they were never mine to keep. My task was to love, cherish, and nurture them into good humans. I hope I've succeeded.

You each love one of my sons . . .

You love them!

Please know that I already love you for that.

Thank you,
Giovanna xx

THE DEATH CHAT

Dear Buzz,

Tonight when I was putting you to bed we had a chat while my head was resting on your chest. I love getting into bed with you boys and having a snuggle at the end of the day – it's the only time each of you can keep still enough for me to do this with you. You're always on the go in the daytime – running, bouncing and climbing. When you're unwinding before bed and we're reading stories or talking about the day, you're all still

and cute, ready to curl up nice and close and let me breathe you in.

Anyway, we were cuddling, and you had your arms wrapped around me in such a fashion that it felt like you were the adult and I was the child, as though the roles had been reversed. I said to you that one day you'll hold me in that exact same way but you'll be a big man and I'll be an old lady. You cried. You sobbed. When I asked what was wrong you said, 'I don't want you to be an old lady. You're my mummy!' Well, that just broke my heart. 'I don't want you to die,' you sobbed, and let out another ginormous wail.

I got it then. That's what we've told you about people like your great-nonna in Italy, or what you've seen in a few films. Old people die. So when I said I would be old one day, you heard and understood it to mean that I would die one day. I tried to explain that everyone dies, that it's something that's going to happen to all of us, but you then asked, 'Will you come back?' your voice giving the tiniest squeak as you delivered the question. Your face was a mixture of hope and dismay as you waited for my reply, knowing the answer but willing me to say something different.

Oh, Buzz . . . your heart has captured mine so wholly.

I told you that we have so many more adventures to

go on together before I get old (although the grey hairs
on my head would suggest otherwise). Then we started
listing them all. *You* cracked some jokes. It was so sweet
watching you go from heartbroken to trying to perk us
both up. In truth, I wanted to tell you that life is shit
sometimes. That I hate the fact that I can't promise you
I'll even make it to old age. That as much as I want to
go on all these adventures with you, I can't guarantee
that either of us will be here to see them all through . . .
but I could never say that to you. Learning about life
and death is part of you growing up and developing a
deeper understanding. Realizing that we are not all
going to be here for ever is part of being a five-year-old.

I'm sorry the mere thought of death shattered your heart tonight. Grief is ugly and raw, and I hate knowing that one day you'll have to experience those emotions for real and not just in the safety of a 'one day' conversation.

All I can say is that I am here, and you are here. Let's make the most of *now*. Let's spend our Sundays eating waffles and going on big bike rides or picnics. Let's spend all your school holidays seeing the world and doing cool stuff like camping, bouncing on trampolines all day long, and planning missions into space. Let's be *together* as a family. Because whatever happens in life you guys will always be the thing that matters the most. *You* are real.

I'm sorry I can't shield you from the heartache of losing a loved one. I'm sorry I can't protect you from leaving this world either.

But I can enjoy the now with you. The now. The now. Let's repeat it, because it's the most important time we have.

I love you, my little sensitive bean!

Your Mumma xxx

To my pregnant friends,

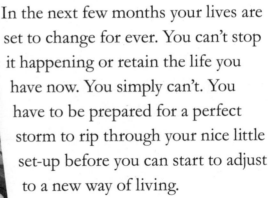

In the next few months your lives are set to change for ever. You can't stop it happening or retain the life you have now. You simply can't. You have to be prepared for a perfect storm to rip through your nice little set-up before you can start to adjust to a new way of living.

But I know you know that . . . right? Or is a tiny part of you thinking along the lines Tom was when we were expecting Buzz? He assumed our newborn would happily slot into the routine and plans we already had.

We weren't foolish, we just didn't know how much such a tiny little thing could take over – physically, emotionally and mentally.

Everyone is going to give you advice, whether you asked for it or not. People will chuck it at you – huge mounds of it will be flying at you wherever you turn. Friends, loved ones, family members, neighbours, co-workers, strangers – they will all be adamant that they can help you simply by imparting their wisdom. You should know that you're extremely lucky to be in the fold of knowing all the mothering secrets. Now that you know, your motherhood journey will be easy. A walk in the park . . .

I mean, it would be that simple, if the advice they're all adamant in delivering wasn't so conflicting. How can you possibly sleep-train your baby because it's the 'best' way to get them to settle, while also co-sleeping so they feel comforted by you? How can you give them a pacifier to reduce the chance of SIDS, but never go near one in case they 'get hooked'? And how about making sure they get on to a schedule and follow strict nap-times, while never waking a sleeping baby?

Friend, I need you to understand something. They know what they're talking about and they're right.

They're all right.

They're right because they found what worked for them, and this is why they're coming at you so forcefully: so that you don't have to go through the same sleepless nights and anxiety – but you will. Because you and your baby are different from them and theirs, and now is your time to try out a few things and find your way.

Your way.

There is no right or wrong. Just what works for you and your baby.

Go forth and experiment. Allow yourself to make mistakes, and understand that everyone else is just blagging their way through. Don't feel you have to

pretend you have all the answers. Just give yourself the time, freedom and space to listen to your maternal instinct and lead with love.

You will be a wonderful mother. If you're reading this in a panic at how you'll fare, then you already are. Because you care.

Bring on the playdates and the chaos!

Love you!
Giovanna xx

THE JUGGLE AND THE STRUGGLE

Dear Boys,

We have a book upstairs called *You Choose* in which each page is dedicated to a different theme of life, like homes, clothes, food, pets and travel. You get to select the life you would like to live, which is great because it

prompts discussions about the choices we make. One of the pages is work-based, and invariably a footballer, rock star or racing-car driver is always chosen. This isn't too surprising as they go hand in hand with the things you love doing, but it does make me think ahead to when you start getting jobs and how your lives will pan out around them.

I've had all sorts of jobs. When I was nine years old I used to 'work' in Nonno's café. (Aunty Giorgie used to do all the hard stuff, like serve customers and make the coffee. I used to clear and clean the tables at a super-slow pace.) Then when I was twelve I started doing odd jobs for an elderly lady who lived around the corner. I mostly polished her brass ornaments and brushed my way through her wig collection, but she gave me a few quid for my efforts so I was more than happy to do whatever she asked. At thirteen years old, things notched up a gear with a proper Saturday job in my local florist. From there I've been a cleaner, worked in an off-licence, in multiple departments at Debenhams, on the bar at a local gym, and chaperoned child actors. It's all been pretty varied and I thank my lucky stars for the work I do now, which, although tricky and stressful at times, feels a lot less like work than those jobs ever did.

Since becoming a mum, however, time spent working is loaded with guilt. Guilt for working when I could be with you, guilt for being with you and having fun when I have deadlines to stick to, guilt for thinking about work when I should be totally absorbed in mum life, guilt for working at night when I should spend the time chatting to your dad and giving our marriage some love. Then there are times when my eye has been taken off the ball and I forget to pack your trainers, your homework, or send you to school with the wrong colour socks. Minor things to some, but I know it's in my remit to be on top of those things, so the guilt sits with me.

And that is the juggle. All the balls are in the air, waiting to be organized and thrown back up before they can crash to the ground and smash to pieces.

I have to be switched on, whether I'm with you guys, at the school gates, settling down to do some writing or in the studio with a podcast guest.

I have to be loving, engaging, charming, compassionate, resilient, supportive, patient, capable and *awake* all the time.

I cannot zone out or disengage.

I recently had an epiphany when out on tour with *Happy Mum, Happy Baby: Live!*. The shows were wedged between two very busy months, with two books to edit and a trek to train for, as well as the general juggle of having three children and a house to run. I found myself saying, 'I've just got to get the

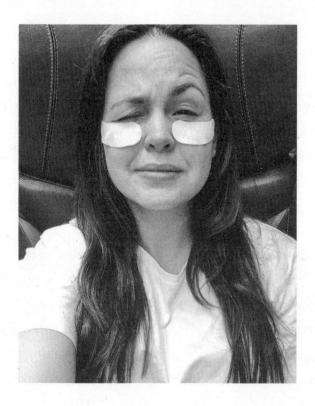

tour out of the way and then I can . . .' An interesting way to think about something I'd worked blooming hard to plan, and was a highlight of my calendar year. It made me question how much of my life I do this with, and I know I'm not the only one doing it. How many days, weeks and months do we just 'get through' in order to reach the next hurdle a little bit quicker?

The ironic thing is that the tour was exactly what I needed. Being surrounded by encouraging humans who just 'got it' made me see that whatever is filling my time in that particular moment should deserve my full attention and care, rather than my mind hopping and skipping on to other things. Of course it's not that I wasn't looking forward to the tour, I absolutely was, but the preparation requires time, and the pressure of the shows running smoothly is all on me. I wanted every audience member to come away feeling lighter and empowered, but I also felt nervous about being away from you boys. I think I was just stressed and apprehensive. It wasn't really because I wanted it to be over.

I know my work situation is unique, but getting through it affects so many people and can prevent us from switching off. Advanced technology has made leaving the office pretty much impossible. Yes, you might shut the doors of your workspace as you leave the building, but work now follows you around. It's in your pocket wherever you go, pulling you in and telling you that if you just send one more work email you'll be able to enjoy your night or weekend more, or that the following week will be easier. It won't. Instead you'll find yourself in the same position, doing the

same thing, but more time will have gone by without you taking time to breathe.

I'm going to start pushing back. Not all the time, but enough to compartmentalize and not feel too bogged down. It might ease the juggling and the guilt, and it might help me enjoy, embrace and immerse myself in whatever I'm doing, without wishing beyond it to the next project.

You will always be my number-one priority and I would gladly stop everything else if you ever needed me to without a second thought. But for now, when I'm working, when I'm away, I'll spend that time focusing on the task in hand and applying myself fully. Yes, I'll coo over the videos and pictures your dad sends and enjoy chatting to you on FaceTime, but my head will be in my work. It doesn't mean I don't care about and love you, simply that if I don't focus and do the best job I can, then I've left you for nothing.

That's the way guilt wins, and there's no way I'm going to let that paralysing emotion overshadow everything else and render it useless.

You are my driving force, so I hope one day you'll look at all I do with pride, knowing you were the ones pushing me forward and helping me knock down everything in my way.

Love you always and for ever,
Mummy xx

EXPECTATION VS REALITY

Dear Boys,

I always wanted to be a mum. My role in any friendship group has always been that of the mother, the one to look after others and put their needs before my own. The one always asking, 'Are you OK?' and trying to make everyone happy.

I have maternal tendencies running through me and I know I am a kind and caring person, but the expectations of what I thought I'd be like as a mother are quite different from reality.

I expected:

- Life to be full of laughter and smiles all year round. I imagined a house full of uncontainable joy, like Santa's workshop, where your dad and I would be jolly and jovial, skipping and dancing with our delightful little elves, who were carefree and cheerful, gleefully singing around our ankles.
- My children to hang off my every word and to listen to everything I had to say.
- To have to say something only once for it to be understood.
- To be like Miss Honey in *Matilda*, gentle, sweet, encouraging and calm.
- To take to 'it' like a duck to water, calmly and serenely floating through my days with my children lovingly holding my hand.
- My children to slip their hands into mine while out and about. Two peas in a pod.
- My children not to throw tantrums, because I would be so in tune with their needs.
- To feel like the luckiest person in the world.

My reality of motherhood is . . .

- It's not all fun and games. Nothing can be light
  and fluffy all the time. We are not like Santa,
  and you are nothing like elves. No one can be
  happy all the time, and parenthood is just like
  any other part of life with its highs and lows.
  There are times when we put music on, dance

and sing, there are times when we're all sitting around laughing, and there are times when I feel so happy I could burst – but it's having the lows that allows the highs to peak and show how wonderful parenthood is. At times.

- That you boys do indeed listen to everything I say, but choose to forget anything of real value but pick up on the bits that interest you or that you shouldn't hear – like me saying, 'Oh, crap,' when I realize we're out of nappies and are in the middle of a poonami explosion, when one of you has puked all over me, or when I simply can't get the coconut-oil lid off the jar and have hungry mouths to feed. We're not F-ing and jeffing all over the place, only when it's warranted, but you pounce on those words, like a cat on a new pair of shoes!

- Sometimes I have to repeat myself over and over and over again, like a fricking parrot. 'Don't jump on the sofa', 'Please don't hit your brother', 'Time to pop your shoes on', 'Can you go and brush your teeth now?', 'Leave your willy alone', 'Leave *his* willy alone . . .' Everything is repeated at least three times, daily, without fail.

- Understanding that Miss Honey is either a saint or a fictional character created to show the brutality and neglect of other characters in the book, but is not actually REAL! She's there for effect. I have friends who are teachers, as well as parents, and they've found it really difficult to have children who don't listen to them at home when thirty children in the classroom do. Especially when pre-kids they would've had a teeny tiny bit of judgement towards other parents. Perhaps it would be interesting to go back to Miss Honey after Matilda moved in and see how that changed their dynamic . . . and whether she's still so gentle and calm.

- There have been times when I haven't felt a natural at motherhood at all. I have questioned myself many times over the choices I'm making and what the knock-on effects are going to be for the adults you'll become. What I have learnt is that I am my biggest critic, and that everyone else is just winging it too.

- That buttons get pushed, testing my patience, and that I often fail. Yet I've learnt that one reaction doesn't overshadow all the others or set a precedent for what's to come. The future is still to be written so I will continue learning, just like you.

- Holding hands can be a huge annoyance for children, especially two-year-olds. You'd rather run away and soar for freedom or throw a huge wobbly at the restriction. There are times you slip into it unknowingly, though, then whip your hand away realizing you'd let your guard down. There is one exception, though, and that is when you're scared or unsure – usually of a dog that's about to come past. On those occasions you've learnt that holding my hand is the perfect remedy for the anxious feeling in your chest and helps you feel safe. In that moment I could give you a thousand kisses for being so cute!

- The role of parent is serious. You have to encourage, teach, discipline and comfort your child. It can be hard work. Some days are harder than others, but the rewards are beyond anything I have felt before.
- A new love has been created. A love like no other that is unique for each child. They say love is blind, but your love for your children seems to shine a light on all that's nonsense, and helps you focus on what is really important.
- That I am one of the lucky ones.

Love you,
Mumma xx

Dear Boys,

I get asked a lot about you and how you differ. I also get asked what I think you'll 'be' when you're older. Hopefully, you'll be respectful, kind, inclusive and giving while snatching up all life has to offer – you know, all the good things any parent wants their children to display (we think it means we did a good job), but when I look to the future you're all doing very different things.

Buzz, you are emotional, dramatic, caring, creative, intelligent, joyful, confident, enthusiastic, considerate, fun-loving and imaginative. I see you on the stage performing, lapping up the crowds and oozing talent. You're a storyteller and love entertaining others.

Buddy, you are explosive, nurturing, adventurous, strong-willed, carefree, gentle, confident, independent, loyal and meticulous. For you I toy between two very different futures, although both carry that streak of independence. Either you're like Bear Grylls and spend your life exploring, on an endless adventure while caring for animals (maybe more Steve Irwin), *or* you're on a constant rave in Ibiza in a straw skirt and fisherman's hat, bouncing around to drum and bass music.

Max, you can moo like a cow, walk and smile a lot. You're the hardest to read, but with your tendency to sit and observe life around you, all with a smile on your face, I'd say you'll be a monk . . .

You are all colourful and complex with many different layers to your personalities. You highlight this by showing different characteristics or interests, all the time ready to explore and discover something new. You watch each other, take in how a brother feels about a new activity, or one they love. You soak up their knowledge like you have a thirst to understand

and analyse, researching the task, testing it to see if you might favour it too.

You are studying life, but there is no real end point in that training. The truth is I'm still discovering who I am. My life meanders and takes me down different paths and avenues – and that is so flipping exciting. Don't feel you have to be one thing and stick to it. Not if it doesn't make you happy. Long gone are the days when you had to pick a career at sixteen years old and stay with it for the rest of your working life. So, Buddy, who knows? You might fulfil both of my predictions. A summer in Ibiza living it large, before going off to see what else the world has to offer.

Ultimately, only you can decide who you will be and what you will do . . . Have fun making that choice!

Love you!
Mumma xx

For Max

I enter the room having heard your call,
Your eyes instantly shining
As a smile pings on to your face,
Your bouncing legs willing me
   to pick up my pace.

The curtains are opened first,
Allowing sunshine to brighten
   the room
Although it was already full of light
For your face is such a golden sight.

Now you're grunting at me,
Your hand bashing on the frame
Of your wooden cot

Just in case I've missed your spot.

I reach out my arms and you leap into them,
Your hands eagerly clambering up to my chest.
No longer can I keep you at arms' length,
For you pull me in with such surprising strength.

You stay there,
Your arms holding on tight,
As though you have been away for weeks
Not just napping those chubby little cheeks.

I stand in your room and hold you close,
Soaking up the moment
And hoping it won't pass too fast,
Hoping you'll always hug me without being asked.

When you do push me away,
A toothy grin now on display,
Your slate-blue eyes start to seek mine,
Then pull me back in – the hold, divine.

IT'S ALL GOT A BIT
HANDMAID'S TALE . . .

To the mum friends,

I have realized that not all of my mates want to discuss a suspected prolapse endlessly or how potty training is going. It doesn't mean they don't love me and aren't there for me but it can get to a point where I know I have to limit the runny-poo chat and go for something that won't put others off their lunch.

I reserve those conversations for you guys. For the baby groups, the chats in the park, the stolen nattering on the tube, the whispered concerns and mutterings at the school gates . . . Yes, I'm aware we sound like Handmaids with our heads in the freezer trying to get out of Gilead. It is a bit like that, although it's my own fret, worry and guilt that I'm trying to escape. It's your reassurance I crave, and you give it in abundance just by listening as we watch our children sucking previously dribbled-on toys and pinching each other's snacks.

When I'm absolutely shattered from a restless night, which might lead to me weeping, you're there. When I want to have a trivial moan about Tom without someone worrying I'm headed for a divorce, you're there. When I want to talk about kids pushing buttons without worrying that the person listening is going to think my kids are little twats, rather than just testing boundaries and learning, you're there.

It's time to get our heads out of that archaic freezer in Gilead and talk openly so that no one feels out of their depth, like they're the only ones doubting themselves or getting it wrong.

I really hope every mother finds a place she feels safe, heard and consoled, whether it's in person or in a thread of conversation she's found online. It's so vital for our maternal mental health that that occurs. Banish the comparisons and fear of being judged. Motherhood is a leveller and we should all be able to understand and feel compassion for one another.

Meet someone to have dozens of unfinished conversations with who won't care if you turn up with regurgitated milk on your shoulder, a messy mum-bun and with a wailing child. Create a bond with someone who won't take offence if you suddenly have to cancel last minute, but instead will check in a few hours later to see if everything is OK.

Be there for each other. We need it.

Praise be,
Giovanna xx

To YOU, the reader,

I've read through this collection of letters and
sobbed. I've been surprised by how crushed I've felt
at times, and how clueless and heartbroken I've been
in those moments. Whenever I'm writing I always go
through an edit reading the pages out loud – it helps
me digest what I've said a little better. Well, I've
struggled to do that this time. The emotion has
lingered in my throat and blocked the sound from
escaping. How can something I always wanted, that I
longed for, cause me to question and doubt myself so
much?

It's because I love my children with all my heart,
and while in any other part of my life 'satisfactory'
might not be the end of the world, I do not want to be
a 'satisfactory' mother. I want to be the best. That is

why it hurts so much to admit when I'm struggling or getting things wrong.

I have wondered if I've kept in too much self-doubt, and whether I should perk it up a bit with a little more fluff and descriptions of the good times, but I think it's peppered with both, and that is the reality of parenthood. The lows exist, but the highs are what make the lows bearable,

no matter how devastating they might feel at
the time.

If you have read these letters and found yourself
identifying with their sentiments, please know that
you are enough. We are enough. And even when the
voice inside tells you, 'This mumma *ain't* got this',
despite what all the slogans on mugs and jumpers
might say, that's OK.

You are not meant to have all the answers, and you
can't possibly be on top of everything all the time.
You are human.

Give yourself a break.

Give yourself some love.

From me to you,
Giovanna xx

ACKNOWLEDGEMENTS

A huge thanks to these fine people who have helped bring this book to life and on to the shelves:

First up my agent Hannah Ferguson, who put her belief in me eight years ago and is always there to offer words of encouragement when needed. Even when I've fallen pregnant and thrown entire schedules, derailing them, she hasn't once batted an eyelid. Hannah, I'm crap at replying to emails, but you know I'll always call when I'm in a pickle! Thanks for just letting me get on with it.

My editor Charlotte Hardman, who previously worked on *Happy Mum, Happy Baby* and has now continued our non-fiction relationship on *Letters on Motherhood*. I have so much trust in Charlotte, and that's so important when I'm handing over words that are so personal. Charlotte, thank you for keeping me on track with your gentle nudging, while never making me feel stressed or pressured! That's quite a skill. And thanks to Charlotte's assistant Amy for all she's done to make things run smoothly.

My MJ publicity and marketing team, Ellie Hughes, Claire Bush and Helena Fouracre – I absolutely love working with you guys and look forward to the mayhem and fun of every publication week. Ellie, bring on the tour. If Laura is coming tell her to bring her running trainers!

Hazel Orme, Nick Lowndes and those who've been entrusted to page proof – thank you for all you've done to ensure these inside pages look good and make sense!

Jon Kennedy, thank you for working your magic on the jacket design.

Rebecca, Claire, Ange and all of the team at YMU – thanks for allowing me to blackout my diary . . . I told you I was actually working and not just wanting extra time off. ;-) Max, Gaby and the ace team at Dundas – thank you for always having my back.

Mum and Dad, thank you for being solid parents and brilliant role models. I already had so much love for you, but writing these letters has made me love you both even more. Thank you for everything you've done for me, Giorgie, Mario, and our children. I hope my kids look to me in the same way that I look to you.

Bob and Debbie, thank you for looking after my children so that I could write about having children . . .

To the mothers (and fathers) in my life who bring me so much wisdom/ridiculousness/laughter online and in the real world – you make me feel like I'm not the only one, and give me the confidence to write books like this. Thank you.

Tom, Buzz, Buddy and Max – the book is in! Let's go relax before I have to go promote it or write another one. In all seriousness, you are my world. Thank you for inspiring me so much and giving me endless material to ponder on. I love you.